Kevin's brain seemed to be on "spin cycle" as Lori clung to him and cried. Do I just stand here with my hands in my pockets? . . . Why would anyone drink and drive? . . . Do I hold her? . . . Why the creepy organ music? . . . What is everyone thinking about us like this? . . . Who invented ties, anyway? . . . Are we holding up the funeral?

Slowly, Kevin pulled his hands out of his pockets and cautiously put his arms around Lori. Immediately she pulled away. "I'm ready to sit down," she announced with composure.

They quickly found two seats in the back row. Though Kevin's mind continued to whirl, he managed to remember enough of the minister's message to quote in his high-school paper's article: "a good student . . . active in Student Council . . . the hardest days are ahead as the reality that you'll never see Brian again in this life over- comes each of you . . . feelings of shock, denial, anger, confusion . . . a day that you are forced to confront your own mortality . . . "

Death & Beyond

Answers to Teens'
Questions about Death,
Reincarnation, Ghosts,
and the Afterlife

JAMES WATKINS

Tyndale House Publishers, Inc.
Wheaton, Illinois

Library of Congress Cataloging-in-Publication Data
Watkins, James, date
    Death & Beyond : answers to teens' questions about death,
reincarnation, ghosts, and the afterlife / Jim Watkins.
        p.   cm.
    ISBN 0-8423-1278-1
    1. Death—Psychological aspects. 2. Death—Social aspects.
3. Disasters—Psychological aspects. I. Title. II. Title: Death
and beyond.
BF789.D4W3155   1993   93-9702
155.9′37′0835—dc20

To my loving wife, Lois,
"'til death do us part."

CONTENTS

Foreword

When I was asked to write the foreword for Jim Watkins' new book, *Death & Beyond,* I was both honored and concerned. This was a book about death! Not your average instructional or motivational material. *How can someone tackle a subject like this? Does Jim Watkins* like *this kinda stuff? Does he expect me to read this before bed?* While thoughts like this were racing through my mind, I was overwhelmed with a need to start reading immediately.

As a teenager, I quickly learned about love, sex, and relationships, but no one ever talked about dying. As dark as the topic seemed, it was one subject I wanted some light shed on. I had a host of questions, many of which were never answered because no one was talking.

Within the pages of *Death & Beyond,* Jim Watkins *is* talking, and through the amount of research he has done, he speaks as an authority. As I finished each chapter I couldn't help but wish this book had been available during my school years. My friends and I had spent many hours discussing topics such as these: "What is death like?" "Why do people have to die?" "Is there really life after death?" Although speculation makes for a healthy conversation, there's no substitute for the facts and real answers to burning questions—and that's what you'll find in this book.

Another thing I really enjoyed about *Death & Beyond* was the fiction section, which centers on four high-school journalism students. The facts of the book never get tedious because Jim brings these characters in at just the right times. After all, what's a good book without a little mystery and romance?

This book is a perfect marriage of a lot of fact and a little fiction. It will answer many of your questions and possibly create some new ones as well. One thing's for sure—it's a must for all of those who have questions about "death and beyond."

Rick Cua

Acknowledgments

Thanks to one thousand teens from northern Indiana for their honest questions about death.

Thanks to the many people who shared answers, not only from their heads, but from their hearts, on the subject of death: intensive care nurses Tina Bowen and Charlene Baungartner; Mike Carlton; school counselor Marge Cavanaugh; police officer Jerry Custer; Charlie and Judy Davis; Anne Root; family practice physician Ron Sloan; funeral directors Jim and Mike Stone; and the ordained minister with whom I share my life, Lois Watkins.

Thanks to my fifteen-year-old daughter, Faith, and her good friend Jenny Grubaugh for their invaluable input as critics of the rough draft.

And thanks to Karen Ball, my editor, whose light-hearted humor kept me writing on such a heavyhearted subject. And to Kathy Stinnette, whose thorough editing caught some really embarrassing mistakes, thanks!

Introduction

"Is there really life after death?"

That question ranked number one when I asked nearly one thousand junior- and senior-high students to complete these two statements:

A question(s) I have about death is:
A question(s) I have about the possibility of life after death is:

The top question was asked by one out of ten students, followed by **"Do you come back as someone or something else?"**

"Why do people have to die?" ranked third.

"What is death like?" and **"Does death hurt?"** tied for the fourth spot.

The last five questions, in order, were: **"Where do you go when you die?" "Are you able to come back as a ghost and haunt people?" "What is heaven like?" "Are there such things as ghosts?"** and **"What is hell like?"**

Several students responded, **"I don't want to think about it."**

Two years ago I surveyed one thousand teens for my book *Sex Is Not a Four-Letter Word.*[1] Since I had been a teen for seven years and have worked with and written for young people for seventeen more years, I wasn't surprised by many of the questions about love and sexuality.

This year, however, I *was* surprised to discover that questions about death prompted more concern from teens than love and sexuality! For instance, a research study in 1980 found that students today are "more pre-occupied with thoughts of death" than young people fifty years ago. And when *Psychology Today* ran a question-naire about sex, the magazine received ten thousand responses. But a survey about death drew three times that many!

Perhaps I shouldn't have been surprised. While dat-ing is a wonderful option for teens, death is an unin-vited, unwelcome intruder that breaks through the door into all our lives. (While I was writing this book, two junior-high and three high-school students were killed in auto accidents, a twelve-year-old died of cancer, a high-school teacher died of a heart attack during class, and a high-school student was killed by a train while walking across the tracks—all in our rural county.)

When I really thought about it, I realized that I started writing about death long before I started writing about sex. As editor of my high-school paper, I wrote an obituary for every issue the first semester.

David, a recent graduate, was killed in action with the Marine Corps.

Another graduate, Jeanie, died of an unexplained illness.

Jim, a junior, died in an automobile accident. (The police suspected suicide.)

"Miss Chip," a phys-ed teacher, died of cancer.

Diana, a freshman, was found brutally murdered in a field next to the school.

Needless to say, these deaths raised many of the same questions I saw on my recent survey. Everything I've included in this book is in response to the questions teens wrote on the surveys. To find the answers I went to people who have confronted this intruder.

I talked with doctors and intensive care nurses as I tagged along during a hospital shift. I spoke with patients who had "out-of-body experiences" while just inches from death. I rode "shotgun" with a police officer who has investigated teen murders and suicides (and who let me read actual suicide notes). A funeral director allowed me to witness the embalming of a body. I interviewed a school counselor who dealt with teens following multiple deaths of their classmates, the parents of a girl who killed herself at fifteen, and a mother who lost a son to AIDS and a daughter to a murderer. And I talked with ministers who attempt to provide answers— or at least hope—during the funerals of young people.

To keep things from getting too depressing, we'll mix in some love and mystery in the lives of four fictional high-school journalism students—Kevin, Kathy, Nate, and Lori—as we wrestle with questions about real-life "slashers," suicide, reincarnation, ghosts, grief, funerals, heaven and hell, how to avoid death (at least for as long as possible), and much, much more.

All the case histories in the nonfiction portions of the book are true, but some of the names and details have been changed for the sake of the survivors.

I realize this book may raise as many questions as it answers. That's why I wish I could sit down and talk with you face-to-face. Books, magazine articles, and letters can be helpful, but they can't address your one-of-a-kind questions.

You need a flesh-and-blood person to give you emotional, social, and spiritual support as well as guidance as you deal with questions about death and dying. I trust there is someone you can talk to about your questions: your parents, a school counselor, a youth worker,

xv

a pastor, or some other trusted adult. I hope you will find the right person to share with.

My hope and prayer is that this book will help you in two ways:

(1) Give you information that will allow you, as much as humanly possible, to live a long, healthy life.

(2) Give you comfort and hope as you deal with family and friends who won't.

PART ONE

What is death like?

*T*he deafening silence assaulted Kevin Farra as he entered Lakeshore High School two weeks before the first day of school. The squeaks of his new sneakers were the only sounds pin-balling through hallways that were usually filled with laughter, joking, locker doors slamming, and warning bells threatening detention in just two minutes.

The senior caught his reflection in the school's trophy case. Three Quill and Scroll trophies for high-school journalism testified to the Lakeshore Sentinel staff's hard work during the past three years. He brushed his blonde sun-bleached hair back as he spotted another reflection.

"How's the new editor?" a familiar voice asked.

"Great," Kevin answered as he swung around to face Lori Reed. Kevin and Lori had grown up in the same neighborhood and had been inseparable as kids. She could outrun, outpitch, outspit, and outfight most of the boys in the neighborhood. Fortunately, she had remained on Kevin's good side and Little League team throughout elementary school. But then in junior high, her family had moved to the far side of town, so she only saw Kevin at school but had still remained his good friend.

"And how's the new . . . new sports editor?" Kevin stammered. He couldn't believe this was the girl who used to pummel him in tackle football. "You've . . . ah . . . changed . . . your hair."

"And I got contacts," she added as she ran her fingers through her newly permed hair. "So you like the change?"

"Ah . . . you look great." Kevin glanced at his watch to change the subject. "I guess we better get to Norman's office or he'll give us another lecture about 'deadlines mean . . .'"

Lori chimed in and they mimicked their journalism teacher, "'. . . cross this line and you're dead!'"

As they walked toward room A-16, Kevin kept glancing at the "new" Lori. Without her glasses her brown eyes looked larger, and the auburn hair that used to hang limp to her shoulders now looked like a shampoo commercial.

"So let's find out about what you characters were up to this summer. And don't leave out any details—unless, of course, your lawyer has warned you not to make any statements to the press," Mr. Norman announced.

The four young people laughed as they sat around the journalism teacher's desk. Mr. Norman was one of the most popular teachers at Lakeshore: he held classes outside, never took attendance, gave people A's if they made a real effort at improving their writing skills, and basically enjoyed irritating "the establishment," as he called the administration.

He leaned back in his chair, loosened his tie, and rolled up his sleeves. "I had an administration committee meeting this morning so I had to dress for success," he said apologetically as he munched on Doritos. "Breakfast," he *explained, indicating the bag. "We'll start with our new editor, Kevin Farra."*

"Well, not much to report. I mowed a lot of lawns, spent a week at camp—"

"One of the those religious camps where you sit around a campfire and sing 'Kum Ba Yah'?" Kathy interrupted.

Kevin rolled his eyes at his assistant editor. This is going to be a long year, *he thought. Kathy Rodriguez was the unofficial spokesperson for every group that she participated in. She had driven Mr. Collins, the biology teacher and Campus Life club sponsor, nearly crazy with her constant questioning about the New Age, reincarnation, and out-of-body experiences. But her curiosity and bloodhound instincts would make her a great assistant editor—if she didn't drive the entire staff crazy.*

"Why don't you tell us about your summer while you're at it, Kathy?" Mr. Norman suggested.

"Well, I got this really neat job at the downtown library cataloging new books on the computerized card catalog."

"What, no out-of-body experiences, Kathy?" Nate joked. Kevin had suggested Nate Latta as feature editor to Mr. Norman to balance Kathy's tendency to be just a bit mystical.

"No, but how 'bout you and Jennifer? I hear you two had some out-of-body experiences at the lake this summer," Kathy shot back.

"Easy, team," Mr. Norman interrupted. "Save all this hostility for the editorial page. I've got some great targets for all this energy."

"Actually," Nate continued, "I was so busy working

5

at Lakeshore Video that I didn't see much of Jennifer or the lake this summer."

"Too bad," the teacher responded. "Now, let's see, Lori, you'll be covering the sports beat. I trust you'll be able to be objective since you'll be covering Bret Randall and the football team."

Lori stared down at her notebook and picked at the corner. "Bret and I broke up this summer," she said quietly.

Lori glanced up and met Kevin's eyes for a split second, and then she stared at her notebook again.

"I'm sorry. I didn't know, Lori," Mr. Norman said with a reddening face. "Well, let's talk about our first issue. What should we deal with?" he asked, reaching for another handful of Doritos.

"How 'bout the nutritional value of the school lunches?" Kathy suggested as she nibbled on a granola bar.

"So what's wrong with the cafeteria food?" Mr. Norman mumbled through a mouthful of chips. "It contains the four basic food groups—sodium, sugar, fat, and preservatives."

"Really, Mr. Norman," Kathy whined. "It's an important issue."

"OK, OK. Just don't advocate that they replace all the good food with that birdseed that you eat," the teacher answered.

Nate jumped in. "I heard that the school's pool doesn't meet the new state health standards."

"Hey, now there's a great story!" Mr. Norman laughed. "A threat to public health and, of course—my favorite—an establishment cover-up! But what do you need to do first?"

The four students spoke out in unison, "Verify, verify, verify."

"Right. I want two reliable sources. Remember, if your mother says she loves you . . ."

"Verify it," the editors responded.

"Speaking of verifying," Lori asked, "has anyone else heard that Brian McCarthy tested HIV-positive this summer?"

"That explains why he checked out a couple books on AIDS this summer," Kathy added. "I can run a check and know every book that every person has checked out in the last year. Pretty cool, huh?"

"That's not even circumstantial evidence," Mr. Norman argued. "But that brings up an interesting question. How do we want to address the AIDS epidemic?"

"Maybe some articles on safe sex," Kathy suggested.

"You mean 'safer' sex," Kevin countered. "Did you read that the New England Journal of Medicine claims that condoms have a 30 percent failure rate in preventing the spread of sexually transmitted diseases? Maybe we ought to cover that angle."

"And what if someone is diagnosed with a full-blown case of AIDS?" Lori asked. "And how do we cover an AIDS-related death?"

Kathy abruptly changed the subject. "Hey, that reminds me. Are we running movie reviews again this year? Everyone's talking about Varsity Death Squad."

"Yeah," Lori agreed. "That's the one where they advertise 'Who will survive the final cut?!'" she said, her voice switching to an imitation of a deep-voiced announcer—"We could use it on the sports page!" Everyone laughed, but Lori continued, "Seriously though, how would we report a death?"

"Good question," Mr. Norman answered. "But it's

just hypothetical—I hope. I've been here ten years, and we've never had to run one obituary—not even a drunk-driving accident."

8 *One week after classes began, the halls of Lakeshore High School were again strangely silent. No laughing. No joking. Even locker doors seemed to close without a sound.*

Students stood around in small groups, stunned. Brian McCarthy had been killed and Renee Roberts seriously injured in a car crash following the first home football game. The news had spread quickly over the weekend, and Monday morning the Lakeshore Sentinel *staff sat in Mr. Norman's office.*

"I guess it's not a hypothetical question anymore," he said softly.

1

How Many Teens Die Each Year?

It's a miracle that I lived to write this book!

As a kid I tried to make rocket fuel out of gasoline. Jumped car ramps with my bike. Tried parachuting off the garage roof with an umbrella. Spent considerable time in the emergency room for assorted stitches. And watched a tornado lift up the neighbor's garage.

In high school I ended up on the bottom of a pile of teens when a wagon tipped over during a hayride. Tried to ride my unicycle with Kim Williams on my shoulders. (We did real well until both of us suddenly wondered, *How do we get off!?* The answer: With a lot of pain!) And rode to school with Cal "I-bet-I-can-take-that-turn-at-sixty" Albright. (We didn't, but we did make a great 360 in the intersection.)

Later, I flew with an Alaskan bush pilot who commented before takeoff, "We're about fifty pounds over weight, but I *think* we can clear those pine trees at the end of the runway." I've ridden with kamikaze pilots turned Detroit taxi drivers; driven through downtown Chicago—at rush hour—during a snowstorm—with a motor home; nearly drowned trying to rescue a teen swimmer (I would have done fine if his friend hadn't panicked and grabbed me around the neck from behind); and I've wrestled with a teen who was trying to commit suicide by jumping off a second-story balcony. Like I said, it's a miracle I'm alive to write a book about death.

And it's a miracle that you're alive to read it! Nearly one-third of all children in the United States die before birth due to abortions.[1,2] (See note 2 on page 253 for more information on the number-one cause of death.)

What's the main cause of teen deaths?

According to recent figures from the *Statistical Abstract of the United States*,[3] the odds of dying at birth are one in 105 for white males and one in 52 for black males; one in 134 for white females, one in 62 for black females. (In other words, one black female baby will die at birth for every 62 black female babies born.)

The odds for dying before we reach our teen years are one in 74 for white males and one in 40 for black males; one in 96 for white females, one in 47 for black females.

So we've overcome some tough odds just to get to this chapter!

The following charts reveal just how teens die each year:

How Many Teens Die Each Year?	MALE	FEMALE
ACCIDENTS	14,200	4,300
MURDER	4,700	1,100
SUICIDE	4,100	800
AIDS	3,651	388
CANCER	1,100	800
HEART	700	400
OTHER DISEASES	49	1,812
TOTAL	28,500	9,600

What Are Your Odds?	MALE	FEMALE
ACCIDENTS	1/ 1,332	1/ 4,292
MURDER	1/ 4,049	1/16,666
SUICIDE	—	—
AIDS	—	—
CANCER	1/16,949	1/23,810
HEART	1/26,315	1/47,619
OTHER DISEASES	—	—
TOTAL	1/ 662	1/ 1,919

Before getting too depressed by these statistics, keep in mind that 99.8 percent of young men from fifteen to twenty-four years of age will *not* die this year; 99.9 percent of young women in the same age range will *not* die this year.

As we can see on the following "odds chart" our chances of dying in an accident are pretty low, and the chance of dying of cancer or heart disease is lower yet.

If you're a black young man between the ages of fifteen and nineteen, you are much more likely to be killed by gunfire than by any other cause of death, according to the National Center for Health Statistics. In Los Angeles and Washington, D.C., the odds against you are one in 444. In New York City your odds are better: one in 1,000.

What are your chances of getting murdered?

In the case of suicide and AIDS, we can pretty much determine our own odds. And as we'll discover in chapter 5, we can dramatically better our chances of living long enough to have the president send us a card on our one-hundredth birthday.

Despite the good odds, however, teens do die—more than thirty-eight thousand in the United States each year! Chances are that not only will you experience the death of an elderly relative, but you'll also be confronted with the death of a teenage friend sometime during junior high or high school.

2

Is Death Like It Is on TV and in the Movies?

$\mathbf{D}$eath is as big at the box office as sex! Of the top fifty money–making movies ever produced, death is the subject of the first ten and figures in at least ten more on the list. Number one, *E. T., The Extra-Terrestrial,* features a dying alien who is brought back to life. The three Star Wars movies, ranking as numbers 2, 3, and 5, resurrected Obi-Wan Kenobi, Yoda, and even Darth Vader, the ruler of the Death Star.

There's no doubt that death is a lively business in Hollywood. During the week I was working on this chapter, *TV Guide* listed these TV and theatrical movies on the tube: *The Annihilation, Blood Hunt, The Dead Zone, Deadlock, Death Spa, Dial M for Murder, Game of Death, Hang 'em High, The Hanging Tree, Headhunter, I Love You to Death, Indiana Jones and the Temple of Doom, The Killing Game, Marked for Murder, Messenger of Death, My Bloody Valentine, Strike 'em Dead,* and *Thrill Kill.*

And during the last "sweeps week," seven made-for-TV movies included the word *murder* in the title. *Killer* was featured four times, *fatal* and *death* three times each, *dead* and *killing* two times each, and *blood, murder, deadly, kills* and *die* were each used once.

But have the movies and TV dealt with the subject of death realistically? Sure, there's more fake blood and latex body parts than twenty years ago, but is that all?

Un-realism

Hell Raisin' is a typical, low-budget, action-adventure flick starring an unknown cast of big-busted, small-town girls and hormone-powered stock-car drivers. In one scene, two cars race down a country lane that dead-ends at the bank of a river. One car skids to a stop while the other plunges into the water. The hero calmly walks away from the sinking car.

That's the scene that played at local drive-in theaters. In reality, the stunt driver didn't walk away. He was killed when a safety cable snapped. But moviegoers never knew that what they saw was an actual death. They merely saw the hero escape another close call with eternity.

Escaping death—and not death itself—is the subject of most Hollywood offerings. And no one defies death better than Indiana Jones, who holds spots 8 through 10 in the top-movie list.

In *Raiders of the Lost Ark,* the adventuring archeologist escapes two poison darts, two murderous trail guides, two tarantulas, three spears, one avalanche, one giant stone "garage door," one giant stone bowling ball, two dozen South American headhunters with arrows and more poison darts, and finally an anaconda. That's just in the first twelve minutes—nine minutes if you don't count the credits.

The original movie, along with its sequels *The Temple of Doom* and *The Last Crusade,* are supposed to be a salute to the Saturday afternoon matinees of fifty years ago. But it's more like today's Saturday morning TV—the indestructible Indiana succeeds in situations where only a cartoon character could survive!

Batman (ranked number 4), the *Beverly Hills Cop* movies (11, 24), *Lethal Weapon* (27), *Rambo* (31), and *Die Hard* (42) all feature heroes with cartoonlike invincibility and an unrealisitic view of life and death.

Silence of the Lambs, the box-office and Academy Award

success (Oscars for best picture, director, actor, actress, and adapted screen play) is both realistic and unrealistic. The psychological thriller features special agent Clarice Starling tracking down "Buffalo Bill," a transsexual serial killer who skins young women to make a dress out of human flesh. With the help of Hannibal "The Cannibal" Lector, the serial killer is caught, but not before Lector has cut the face off a police officer to use as a mask to escape. The police work and autopsy procedures are agonizingly accurate, but then the final scenes are reduced to the the typical death-defying danger.

15

Even the many "slasher" films, such as *Friday the Thirteenth, Nightmare on Elm Street,* and all their sequels, are unrealistic despite being incredibly graphic.

The ultimate denial of death, however, may be the rumored (at the time of this writing) resurrection of Superman. As I'm writing this chapter, "Doomsday" has sent Clark Kent into the superhero hereafter. But don't expect the man of steel to rust in a Kryptonian crypt for long. DC Comic editor Mike Carlin confesses, "Never say *never.* Never say we wouldn't kill Superman; never say we wouldn't bring him back."[1]

Perhaps it is our fear of death—and our desire to beat it the way our heroes do—that makes TV shows and movies about overcoming death so popular. (We'll talk about our strong desire to deny death in chapter 6.)

Sur-realism

Some presentations of death go beyond *un*real to *sur*real—using fantasy or dreamlike images—in glamorizing death. If we can't defeat death as an enemy, we can attempt to make it a friend.

Flatliners offers a surrealistic look at the beyond as medical students deliberately cause each other to have near-death experiences. (We'll talk about out-of-body experiences in chapter 14.)

Ghost (ranked number 15) presents death as simply leaving one's body and entering a wonderful world of light and music. And, as the amazed medium discovers, people can return from the dead and possess others' bodies. (We'll discuss ghosts in chapter 15 and communicating with the dead in chapter 16.)

Some heavy-metal music groups go beyond glamorizing death to glorifying suicide. Ozzy Osbourne's "Suicide Solution" shouts, "Where to hide, suicide is the only way out." Metallica's "Fade to Black" cries out, "I have lost the will to live. Simply nothing more to give. There is nothing more for me. Need the end to set me free."[2] (We'll discuss suicide in chapter 8.)

Some groups go so far as to glorify murder and human sacrifice themes.

Ice-T's controversial "Cop Killer" raps, "I got my twelve-gauge sawed off. I got headlights turned off. I'm about to dust some cops off. Cop Killer, but tonight we get even."

The heavy-metal group Venom on its *Possessed* album includes the song "Sacrifice"—a virtual how-to for occult sacrifice: "Plunge the dagger in her breast. I insist S-A-C-R-I-F-I-C-E!" Slayer, another heavy-metal group, features the song "Altar of Sacrifice" on their *Rain and Blood* album, which advocates "spilling pure virgin blood."[3] (We'll get inside the minds of murderers in chapter 7.)

Again, our incredible desire to avoid the fear of death causes some to befriend death.

Realism

Walt Disney was one of the first moviemakers to allow his heroes to die. They shot Old Yeller and Bambi's mother!

The producers of the movie *My Girl* were nervous

when Macaulay Culkin, who played the indestructible hero in *Home Alone,* was cast as a bee-bitten corpse in this film. Many felt that it was too "realistic" for what was billed as a young teen film. Other critics complained about the movie *Hook* when the leader of the Lost Boys was killed by Captain Hook. And yet, real heroes do get killed. As we discovered in the last chapter, teens do die.

The publishing world has also discovered that dealing realistically with death is needed. Lurlene McDaniel's best-selling teen novels (*Good-bye Doesn't Mean Forever, Mourning Song, Six Months to Live, A Time to Die, Too Young to Die*) deal with teens facing terminal illnesses and, in one book, a father's suicide. (New books, in what some call the "ten hankie" series, are scheduled to come out every other month.)

The author explains, "Some of them read my novels for entertainment, and some of them read them because they can truly identify with the plot. Even if a youngster doesn't have cancer, she may have had something else very sad happen to her."[4]

Other authors target teens with the Fear Street series: *Suicide's Ghosts; The Vampire Diaries I, II,* and *III; Violent Killer;* and *Whisper of Death.*

The reality of death has also come to music and MTV. Shakespear's Sister's video "Stay," which uses respirators and heart monitors as props, features the singer's tug-of-war with another woman, dressed as death, over her boyfriend.

Eric Clapton's "Tears in Heaven" soared to number 2 on Billboard's charts. The song, inspired by the death of the singer/songwriter's four-year-old son, asks, "Would you know my name if I saw you in Heaven? Would it be the same if I saw you in Heaven?"

Boyz II Men's a capella version of "It's So Hard to Say Good-bye to Yesterday" was first heard at the graveside scene in the movie *Cooley High.*

Perhaps the most realistic portrayals of death began, not in Los Angeles boardrooms, but in the jungles of Southeast Asia. During the late sixties and seventies, the Vietnam War was served with dinner in homes across America. This was the first "live" prime-time TV war: no actors, no exploding red-dye packets, no camera special effects—just the raw images of the horrors of war beamed into our living rooms. Some argue that the televised bloodshed of Vietnam actually turned Americans against that costly war.

While the recent Persian Gulf War was also brought to us live, it was fought with "smart bombs" and "laser-guided missiles" with very few casualties on the Allied side, which may explain the war's support.

Even more shocking—and realistic—are the video-taped deaths chronicled in the documentary *Faces of Death* and its three sequels. Narrated by Dr. Francis B. Gross (what an appropriate last name), the original contains 105 minutes of animal and human death of all dimensions. There are videotaped executions by beheading, electric chair, and gas chamber (we'll talk about capital punishment in the notes for chapter 4—see page 255); autopsies and embalmings (we'll witness an embalming in chapter 9); police photos of murders and accidents; TV coverage of a man committing suicide by dousing himself with gasoline and then setting himself on fire; and much more gore.

Even these "realistic" portrayals of death are commercialized and sensationalized, though. The jackets of the *Faces of Death* quartet look more like slasher movies than like public broadcasting presentations!

In the next chapters, I'll try to present a realistic view of the various dimensions of death. (And I'll try to be truthful without being gruesome.)

PART TWO

Why do people have
to die ?

I just can't believe it! I mean I just ate lunch with Brian and Renee Friday, and now Brian's—" Lori stopped mid-sentence and wiped her eyes with a Kleenex. *"I just can't believe it. . . ."*

The entire staff sat in silence until Nate dared to ask, *"Anyone know for sure what really happened? The city paper was pretty vague. Just that Brian and Renee had been drinking, and that they hit a tree at eighty miles per hour."*

"Rumor has it that Brian had just found out he had AIDS, and Renee was afraid she had gotten it from him," Kathy offered. *"So maybe it was a double suicide."* Kevin saw Mr. Norman raise a suspicious eyebrow. *"I know, I know,"* she added. *"It's not verified."*

"Well, I know this isn't verification, but I drove past where the accident happened, and there aren't any skid marks, so maybe they did do it deliberately," Kevin put in. Even though he'd seen the scraped-up tree, what had happened still seemed too unreal. Speaking of it had a detached emotional feel—sort of like a hypothetical writing assignment.

Just then the phone rang. *"Journalism office, this is Mr.*

Norman. . . . Hey, thanks for returning my call. . . . Yeah. . . . Point one-eight for Brian McCarthy; point one-three for Renee Roberts . . . " Mr. Norman jotted on a spiral dictation pad.

After a few moments, the teacher put down his pen. "No, I'd rather have it on the record. . . . OK, off the record if that's the only way I'm gonna get it. . . . Oh . . . yeah . . . Both of them . . . Yeah, yeah, it's off the record. . . . Hey, I'm not gonna break confidence with a great source. . . . Yeah . . . Thanks."

"So both of them were legally drunk?" Kevin asked as Mr. Norman hung up.

"Yeah. Here's the rest of the information, Kevin. Brian died instantly of massive head and internal injuries. Renee is in critical condition at Community Hospital—head and internal injuries. Neither one of them was wearing a seat belt. Why don't you dig up some background on Brian—school clubs, extracurriculars—for a front-page obituary. The drinking is a part of the story, but don't overplay it."

"Did Deep Throat confirm or deny the AIDS angle?" Kathy quizzed.

"You've been reading the Watergate scandal books again, haven't you?" Mr. Norman answered. "I have no comment for the press, Miss 'Woodward.' "

"But what was the 'off the record' and 'both of them' about?" Kathy pressed.

"Like I said, it's off the record."

"So you won't confirm or deny that Brian and Renee both had AIDS."

"Look, even if we had an on-the-record source to confirm it, I wouldn't let it run. I don't think that's something the public has a right to know," Mr. Norman answered.

Kevin was surprised to find he was offended by Kathy's cold-blooded questioning. Maybe the reality of Brian's death was beginning to sink in. Kathy's interrogation was interrupted by the principal's voice over the classroom speaker.

"Good morning, students," Mr. Coldwater said with his usual lack of expression. "Lakeshore High School regrets to inform you that Brian McCarthy, sixteen, was killed in an automobile accident Friday night. Those wishing to be excused for the funeral at one o'clock Tuesday at the Lakeshore Chapel may sign out in the office." Click.

"That's it? A student is killed, and that's all the school does?" Lori blurted out.

"Probably all the more reason to give this story some major coverage," Mr. Norman responded. "So, Kevin, you cover the hard news angle—give 'em who, what, where, why, and how on Brian's death and Renee's injuries. Why don't you cover the funeral as well? I don't want a transcript of the message, but pull out a couple of significant points. Nate, I want student reaction—questions, feelings, et cetera. Lori, I want you to check with the Central school system. I heard some good things about how they handled the deaths of those three students last year. Check with Lakeshore Mental Health, too, and get some of their ideas on how this should have been handled. Let's put that on the editorial page. Kathy, I'll need you to keep on top of the other news. We're going to have to work fast, but that's the fun of working a real paper—the tight deadlines get the ink in my veins flowing again."

Kevin slowly walked to his next class. Usually the excitement of writing and publishing got the ink pumping in his veins too, but instead, his arteries felt like they were

23

full of Novocain that deadened his whole body. Not even the smell of his favorite school lunch—pizza burgers— could penetrate his brain as he passed the cafeteria.

24 *"So what do you have for me?" Mr. Norman asked at the Tuesday morning 'budget meeting' where stories were reviewed and assigned page positions. "Hello—is anybody home?" he asked when the staff didn't respond. All eyes were focused on his morning snack.*

"Oh, you're wondering about the rabbit food," he said as he munched on carrot sticks. "My doctor says my cholesterol is over three hundred and that I'm a heart attack just waiting to happen. So I'm walking two miles every day and trying to knock off the junk food. Mostly though, I'm trying to stay off the obituary page."

The staff sat in silence.

"Maybe not the best choice of words," the teacher said apologetically. "Brian's death has been really hard to handle, hasn't it?"

The four editors continued to sit in silence until Kevin pulled out his reporter's notebook.

"I talked with Renee's parents, and it doesn't look good for her." He paused as his words seemed to shake the room. "They're not picking up any brain waves, and they're planning to do some kind of 'flow test,' where they shoot radioactive stuff into her bloodstream to see if any blood is getting to her brain. Oh, and Lori's going to help me cover the funeral."

Kathy and Nate exchanged smiles and raised eyebrows.

"It's not a date!" Kevin answered, glancing at Lori. He thought she looked either hurt or embarrassed.

Mr. Norman seemed to sense it, too, so he tried to get

the conversation back on the subject. "OK, Kevin, keep in touch with Renee's parents. Why don't you get some background on Renee just in case . . ." The teacher's voice trailed off. Mr. Norman was always talking about good reporters needing tough hides and tender hearts, but it seemed to Kevin that their journalism teacher was starting to feel the impact of the death. "Ah," Mr. Norman continued after an awkward pause, "what do you have, Nate?"

"Well, the main question is a great big why. Why did it happen? Why do teens have to die when they should have a whole, long life ahead of them? Some students are blaming God for not sparing Brian's life."

"Sounds like you've done some good legwork, Nate," Mr. Norman responded. "What do you have, Lori?"

"Well, I talked with one of the guidance counselors at Central. She said they started off with an assembly where someone from Lakeshore Mental Health talked about the grief process, and then they broke up into small groups to talk about the students' questions. Some people from Lakeshore Mental Health helped lead those discussions. I also got some reactions from kids who thought Mr. Coldwater was pretty insensitive with his life-goes-on attitude."

"Sounds good," Mr. Norman complimented. "Just keep it balanced. Be sure to talk to Mr. Coldwater and get his rationale for doing it the way he did. OK, team, let's get out there and report some news."

The Lakeshore Chapel was like any of the family-owned funeral homes overlooking Main Street in small towns throughout the Midwest: a white-sided house that had been remodeled, added on to, re-remodeled, and added on to again and again.

Standing outside, however, Kevin thought it looked more like a West Coast bikers' rally. Apparently the two hundred or more high-school students who came for the funeral had gone to their closets and pulled out anything black: black leather jackets, black sweatshirts, black jeans, and black T-shirts with heavy-metal music group logos. The teens stood in small groups across the yard and sat on car hoods. Only the wind and birds in the elm trees and an occasional car on Main Street broke the eerie silence. It reminded Kevin of the deathly stillness prior to a violent thunderstorm.

Kevin and Lori also stood in silence—not sure what to say to each other or to those around them. Lori wiped away an occasional tear. Usually Kevin felt comfortable being with Lori, but he felt his tie tighten around his neck as he tried to think of something to say or do to comfort her. This tie must be cutting off the blood to my brain, *he thought.*

Kevin was glad that he and Lori had arrived a half hour early since the small funeral home was nearly at its fifty-person capacity. The funeral director motioned in groups of five at a time, then would close the door until they were seated. The door finally opened one more time, and Kevin and Lori were ushered onto the remodeled porch and then into what must have once been the living room. In the corner a bronze-colored casket was draped with flower arrangements. Three girls were huddled at the head of the casket, blocking Kevin's view of Brian's body.

"Ah, do you want to see—" Kevin stopped abruptly to avoid making a decision whether to say Brian *or the* body. What do you call the body? *Kevin wondered.*

"Yeah, I'd like to see Brian one more time."

The two slowly—cautiously—moved closer to the casket. Students had brought Brian's favorite tapes, CDs, and magazines and cans of his favorite soft drink— Dr Pepper—to leave in the casket. A small stuffed teddy bear sat at his waist.

Kevin was shocked at Brian's appearance. The heavy makeup must be covering up black and blue marks on his swollen face, *he thought.*

Lori reached over the edge of the casket and touched Brian's hand. Why would anyone want to touch a dead body? *Kevin asked himself. He wanted to get to his seat, get the funeral over, and get this noose of a tie from around his neck. But Lori just continued staring at Brian.*

Suddenly, without warning, she turned from the casket, buried her face in Kevin's chest, and began to sob. Kevin stood, stunned, with his hands in his pockets. What should I do? *he thought.*

3
What's the Cause of Death?

Bill sits beneath the blinding lights of the TV studio. The skin on his face hangs like the rippled curtains behind him, and spotlights reflect off his bald head. He pushes himself back in the chair with thin, wrinkled arms and hands and then rubs his back, which is disfigured with arthritis. As he begins to talk, his voice is weak and sometimes hard to understand due to several missing teeth. Bill is twelve years old!

Yes, twelve. He's a guest on a talk show featuring a little-known disease called Werner's Syndrome—premature aging. Bill's body will race through childhood, adolescence, and old age within two or three decades. He'll probably die of "old age" before forty. ***Why do people die?***

Doctors and researchers are particularly anxious to learn what causes this rare form of aging. And if they can, they may be able to answer the age-old question, Why do we die?

Theories of why we fall apart fall into two parts:

Wear and Tear
Our cells busily reproduce themselves throughout our lifetime. During all this multiplying and dividing of protein, our DNA (the genetic blueprint) occasionally

makes a mistake. Scientists speculate that exposure to toxins (poisons in our environment), chemicals, and ultraviolet light breaks, twists, or scrambles these genetic codes. And thus occasional "factory defects" roll off our cell assembly lines.

30

When enough bad products accumulate, cells begin to break down, and our bodies begin to show signs of aging. The chart below shows how our bodies lose efficiency over the years. At 100 percent efficiency our bodies would be working perfectly at maximum power; at zero percent—well, you wouldn't be reading this book.

AGE	25	45	65	86
MUSCLES	100%	90%	75%	55%
HEART	100%	94%	87%	81%
LUNGS	100%	82%	62%	50%
KIDNEYS	100%	88%	78%	69%
CHOLESTEROL	198	221	224	206

Now you know why there are so few professional athletes over forty! With age, athletes—and everyone else—lose muscle strength and lung capacity as well as experience decreasing heart and kidney effectiveness.

Gooey, sticky sugar

One cause of wear and tear may be blood sugar called *glucose*. High levels of glucose can cause protein cells to stick together in a gooey mess. These globs of protein and glucose can cloud over our eyes, clog arteries, gum up kidney functions, and make breathing difficult.

Scientists discovered this suspect in the aging process while studying diabetics. Diabetics have higher-than-normal blood sugar levels and one-third lower life expectancy than nondiabetics. (Incidentally, switching to NutraSweet or giving up sugar altogether has no observable effect.)

Mice and rats that were fed 40 percent fewer calories than the rodents in neighboring cages at the National Toxology Laboratory lived twice as long. Physiologist Edward Masoro believes the slimmer diet produced less glucose, thus less goo, and finally less chance of premature death.[1]

Our body's immune system produces cells called *macrophages,* which are sent out on seek-and-destroy missions against these sticky glucose bonds. The dieting rats also had more of these macrophage goo chewers. But, for some yet-unknown reason, these goo gobblers become less efficient as we age.

Rust and "radicals"

Not only do we get sticky and gooey, we also rust with age! Oxygen and "free radicals" allegedly cause protein to rust much the same way the elements cause a car to fall apart.

Free radicals were first discovered by Denham Harman of the University of Nebraska. The burning of oxygen in cells produces these mutant molecules that stalk our bodies, destroying fats and proteins. Exposure to sunlight, X rays, ozone, tobacco smoke, and air pollution are also suspects in the creation of those molecular muggers.

Harman's fellow researchers blame free radicals for destructive diseases such as arthritis, diabetes, hardening of the arteries, heart and kidney failure, lung disease, and even cancer.

Planned Obsolescence

Planned obsolescence means that a product is designed to self-destruct in a certain number of years. (Have you noticed that as soon as your CD player's warranty expires, so does your CD player?) Some researchers believe that our bodies are made the same way—we are programmed to self-destruct after seventy years.

And despite modern science, people are not living any longer than this genetic "guarantee" allowed people to live centuries ago. Today more people are simply living.

For instance, if two people die at birth and two people live to be seventy, then the average life span is thirty-five. If only one person dies in infancy and three reach seventy, the life expectancy jumps to fifty-two. And if all four make it to retirement, then the average life span soars to seventy! But not one person has lived any longer—more have just lived to reach seventy.

What's the longest you can live? Scientists claim that the longest possible life span is between 115 and 120. But that's nothing new: the book of Genesis states the limit is "a hundred and twenty years" (Genesis 6:3, NIV). (We'll talk about 969-year-old Methuselah later.) The ancient Roman Pliny the Elder wrote about one-hundred-year-old people. Shigechiyo Izumi of Japan, the oldest person in recent history, lived to the ripe old age of—you guessed it!—120.

According to recent statistics, guys born in 1990 can expect to live to 76.1 years and girls to 83.4, with many living long enough to receive a one-hundredth-birthday card from the president.

But why can't we break the 120-year barrier? Scientists claim the answer is genetics. And since identical twins, who have identical genes, have very similar natural life expectancies, scientists claim that we are programmed by our DNA to self-destruct at a certain age.

In the same way that our bodies change during adolescence, some researchers believe we begin to fall apart on some genetic cue.

For instance, between the ages of fourteen and seventy our immune system—which fights off disease—decreases by 90 percent. Microbiologist Leonard Hayflick is even more fatalistic. In 1964 he discovered that human cells seem to divide only fifty times and then die. Fifty times and no more!

Others, like the University of Colorado's Thomas Johnson, believe that the exact gene for long life can be isolated. Right now his research is with worms, but he believes he has located the gene that makes the difference between long- and short-lived fish bait.

UCLA researcher Roy Walford may be the first genetic engineer to lengthen life. He's attempting to transfer genes from eight-year-old mice into shorter-living rodents.

"It came from outer space"

If 120 years seems to be the maximum life span for humans, how do we justify biblical accounts of people living nearly a thousand years? The fifth chapter of Genesis claims Adam lived to celebrate 930 birthdays. And Methuselah had 969 candles on his cake!

Here's an interesting theory: In the Creation story it appears that earth was covered with a greenhouse covering of water. "'Let there be an expanse between the waters to separate water from water.' So God made the expanse and separated the water under the expanse from the water above it. And it was so. God called the expanse 'sky'" (Genesis 1:6-8, NIV). It appears that high above the sky a shield of water protected the earth from the sun's radiation.

How come people lived longer in the Bible?

In the Flood story, the author reports "all the springs of the great deep burst forth, and the floodgates of the heavens were opened" (Genesis 7:11, NIV).

As we noted earlier, the sun's ultraviolet rays are thought to be a factor in the aging process. Is it possible that this "radiation shield" came crashing down from the

33

heavens? Without the protection, it only makes sense that we could expect much shorter life spans.

Sure enough, the life spans begin to fall in future chapters of Genesis: Noah's son Shem lived to be "only" 500; Abraham lived to be 170; Joseph lived to be 110.

It appears that the aging process is a result of both wear and tear and planned obsolescence. But we don't need to be fatalistic—"When my number's up, my number's up!" Diet, exercise, and other factors that we'll discuss in chapter 5 can delay the dying process.

4

Who Decides Who Dies?

Teen Convicted of Beating Friend to Death
Teen Daughters Admit Killing Their Mother
Boy Pleads Guilty to Killing His Sister
Gun Killings among Teens Triple in Some Areas
Inmate Executed for Holdup That Led to Death
    of Three
Rapists Executed by Lethal Injection
Study Sees Vast Spread of AIDS by 2000
Former "Marlboro Man" Dies of Lung Cancer
"Doctor Death" Counseled Woman before She
    Committed Suicide
Drinking Suspected in Death of Two Teens
Three Teens Die in Auto Accident
Bungee-Jump Owners Charged with Death of
    Operator
Two Die as Tornadoes Rip through Three Counties
Three Teens Crushed to Death at Rock Concert
Amnesty International Reports Annual Casualties
    of Wars around World
71 Feared Dead in Airline Crash

These are just a few of the articles I clipped out as I researched this book. (I decided against clipping out all the health-related deaths and finally stopped clipping out alcohol-related fatalities and murders not committed by teens. Otherwise we *never* would have gotten through them all.)

Some of the people died from events completely beyond their control: victims of murders, war, drive-by shootings, airline crashes, and natural disasters. (Some New Age followers and reincarnationists, however, believe even these victims *chose* to die.)

Others died from events that they had some control over: smokers, drunk drivers, those engaging in intravenous drug use or unsafe sex. Although they never intended to end their lives, their habits contributed to their deaths. (We'll talk more about this in the next chapter.) Death-penalty supporters argue that convicted criminals make a choice to commit capital crimes and thus make themselves liable to execution.[1] (See note 1 on page 255 for another way to look at capital punishment.)

Does God take people's lives?

Those who commit suicide would seem to have complete control over their deaths, but that may not always be the case. (We'll discuss this further in chapter 8.)

So who decides who dies and when?

Reincarnationists argue that it's *karma*. (We'll discuss this in chapter 17.)

Others feel it's fate: "When your number's up, your number's up."

Some believe that God controls our destiny. But even that idea brings up more questions than it answers.

Why would an almighty God put us on earth so that we are just going to die and put our family through that?

Why does death happen at the worst possible time?

Why does God have to take away loved ones when it seems like you really need them here on earth at this time?

Why does God create disease that's meant to punish people, such as AIDS, but the disease kills innocent people?

I've always been confused about something. I'm pretty sure (not positive) it says in the Bible that God knows our fate before we're ever born. Why then would it make a difference what you do in life? If we're predestined, we have no control, right?

These questions are as old as Job, which is possibly the oldest book of the Bible. This godly man lost his children, his health, and his considerable wealth. For thirty-six chapters Job and his three friends try to answer the haunting question of *why*. But the answer never comes. Instead, God thunders out even more questions:

Why are you using your ignorance to deny my providence? Now get ready to fight, for I am going to demand some answers from you, and you must reply. Where were you when I laid the foundations of the earth? Tell me, if you know so much. (Job 38:2-4)

Stand up like a man and brace yourself for battle. Let me ask you a question, and give me the answer. Are you going to discredit my justice and condemn me so that you can say you are right? Are you as strong as God, and can you shout as loudly as he? (Job 40:7-9)

Then Job replied to God:

I know that you can do anything and that no one can stop you. You ask who it is who has so foolishly denied your providence. It is I. I was talking about things I knew nothing about and did not understand, things far too wonderful for me. (Job 42:1-3)

The apostle Paul agrees with Job:

Oh, what a wonderful God we have! How great are his wisdom and knowledge and riches! How impossible it is for us to understand his decisions and his methods! (Romans 11:33)

May you be able to feel and understand . . . how long, how wide, how deep, and how high [God's] love really is . . . though it is so great that you will never . . . fully know or understand it. (Ephesians 3:18-19)

So, at the risk of writing about things we don't "understand" and "things far too wonderful" for us to comprehend, let's look at these clues.

Providence

Providence simply means "control." Throughout Scripture we read that God has absolute control over his creation:

I know that you can do anything and that no one can stop you. (Job 42:2)

For [God] is in the heavens and does as he wishes. (Psalm 115:3)

O Lord God! You have made the heavens and earth
by your great power; nothing is too hard for you!
(Jeremiah 32:17)

God is interested in the well-being of his cosmic creation,
but he seems even more interested in his human creations.
The psalmist thanks God:

Thank you for making me so wonderfully complex!
It is amazing to think about. Your workmanship is
marvelous—and how well I know it. You were there
while I was being formed in utter seclusion! You saw
me before I was born and scheduled each day of my
life before I began to breathe. Every day was recorded in your book! (Psalm 139:14-16)

It appears that God is active in each of our activities.
And somehow he has "numbered" our days on this planet.

Paul writes, "And we know that all that happens to us
is working for our good if we love God and are fitting into
his plans" (Romans 8:28). This certainly doesn't imply that
God keeps bad things from happening to those who love
him, but somehow—in his providence—he does bring
good out of a bad situation.

In the opening chapters of Job, God puts a limit on the
plans that Satan has for Job. Similarly, we are
told in 1 Corinthians 10:13 that when we **_Why is_**
face problems and temptations, we "can trust
God to keep the temptation from becoming **_there death?_**
so strong that [we] can't stand up against it,
for he has promised this and will do what he says."

So God does seem to have things pretty well under
control. But you say, If God is so powerful and personal,
why isn't this heaven on earth? Why is there death? Why is
there disease? Why is there evil?

The book of Psalms is filled with such questions. "My God, my God, why have you forsaken me? Why do you refuse to help me or even to listen to my groans? Day and night I keep on weeping, crying for your help, but there is no reply" (Psalm 22:1-2).

The answer is found in one of the most incredible characteristics about this all-powerful God—he gave us the gift of choice. "Decide today whom you will obey" (Joshua 24:15).

Isn't AIDS a punishment from God?

We can bow down to him or turn our back on him. We can praise him or curse him. And most outrageous of all, we can love him or nail him to a cross and crucify him!

But does this mean that anything bad—including death—that happens to us is a result of our personal disobedience? For instance, at a teen's funeral, the pastor announced, "John was killed because he sinned." Others have claimed that AIDS is a punishment from God. Let's look at what Jesus said about tragedies:

About this time [Jesus] was informed that Pilate had butchered some Jews from Galilee as they were sacrificing at the Temple in Jerusalem.

"Do you think they were worse sinners than other men from Galilee?" he asked. "Is that why they suffered? Not at all! . . .

"And what about the eighteen men who died when the Tower of Siloam fell on them? Were they the worst sinners in Jerusalem? Not at all!" (Luke 13:1-5)

Many times the tragedies of life are not the result of personal disobedience to God, but the result of the rebellion we find recorded in Genesis chapter 3. The perfect creation became marred with disease and death:

For all creation is waiting patiently and hopefully for that future day when God will resurrect his children. For on that day thorns and thistles, sin, death, and decay . . . will all disappear, and the world around us will share in the glorious freedom from sin which God's children enjoy.

For we know that even the things of nature, like animals and plants, suffer in sickness and death as they await this great event. . . . We, too, wait anxiously for that day when God will give us our full rights as his children, including the new bodies he has promised us—bodies that will never be sick again and will never die. (Romans 8:19-23)

While God will eventually punish those who reject his offer of salvation (see chapter 21), the New Testament is clear that "he is not willing that any should perish" (2 Peter 3:9). Any "judgment" that occurs now comes from the natural consequences of our behavior, and not from God.

AIDS, for instance, is transmitted by blood-to-blood or blood-to-semen contact (see chapter 5). So those who engage in practices that promote these conditions will be hardest hit, not because of divine justice, but because of natural consequences. Thus, homosexual males and intravenous drug users who shared needles were the primary carriers of the disease in the United States. Heterosexuals are now the fastest-growing group of AIDS carriers.

If God has set the date of our death, what difference does it make how we live?

It appears, then, that God does have control over our life and our death: "Every day [is] recorded in [his] book!" (Psalm 139:16). But he has also given us free will to make choices that prolong our life or shorten it. That sounds contradictory! But the Bible is filled with concepts that don't make sense to our finite mind: God is three (the Father, the Son, and the Holy Spirit) and yet one! Jesus Christ was 100 percent God and 100 percent human! Don't ask me to explain it! I've simply stuffed these ideas in my mental file folder labeled "Things I'll Never Understand on Earth."[2]

So while God *knows* our date of death before our birth, he in no way *causes* our death. Perhaps it will be cancer, a drunk driver, a murderer, defective brakes on our car, a tornado or earthquake, an airplane crash, or one of a thousand different causes—but it won't be God. (See chapter 5.)

This still leaves lots of questions about . . .

Justice

Why do innocent people get killed by drunk drivers who walk away unharmed? Why do drug dealers live like kings while God-fearing families live on food stamps? There doesn't seem to be a lot of justice, yet God is supposed to be so just!

One of the writers of Psalms struggled with these same questions.

> For I was envious of the prosperity of the proud and
> wicked. Yes, all through life their road is smooth!
> They grow sleek and fat. They aren't always in
> trouble and plagued with problems like everyone
> else, so their pride sparkles like a jeweled necklace,
> and their clothing is woven of cruelty! These fat cats
> have everything their hearts could ever wish for!
> They scoff at God and threaten his people. How
> proudly they speak! They boast against the very
> heavens, and their words strut through the earth.
>   And so God's people are dismayed and confused

and drink it all in. "Does God realize what is going on?" they ask. "Look at these men of arrogance; they never have to lift a finger—theirs is a life of ease; all the time their riches multiply."

Have I been wasting my time? Why take the trouble to be pure? All I get out of it is trouble and woe—every day and all day long! (Psalm 73:3-14)

Do you ever feel that way? Does living for God seem like a waste of time?

"Brandon's dad is an alcoholic, but my dad's dead thanks to a drunk driver!"

"I prayed for my only grandmother, but she died anyway. Carla's the biggest slut at school, and yet both her grandmothers are still living!"

"Some big-time crime boss dies at eighty years old, and yet my pastor died of a horrible cancer at forty-five!"

Where's this justice the Bible talks about? The second half of the psalm gives us the answer:

It is so hard to explain . . . this prosperity of those who hate the Lord. Then one day I went into God's sanctuary to meditate and thought about the future of these evil men. What a slippery path they are on— suddenly God will send them sliding over the edge of the cliff and down to their destruction: an instant end to all their happiness, an eternity of terror. Their present life is only a dream! They will awaken to the truth as one awakens from a dream of things that never really were!

When I saw this, what turmoil filled my heart! I saw myself so stupid and so ignorant; I must seem like an animal to you, O God. But even so, you love me! You are holding my right hand! You will keep on guiding me all my life with your wisdom and counsel, and afterwards receive me into the glories of heaven! (Psalm 73:16-24)

We often do "reap what we sow" in this life as the natural consequences of our behavior. But God's love for his creation causes him to put off divine justice for as long as possible: "He is waiting, for the good reason that he is not willing that any should perish, and he is giving more time for sinners to repent" (2 Peter 3:9).

On Judgment Day, justice will finally roll. But until then, God is giving everyone a chance to accept his offer of forgiveness.

That still doesn't answer every question. But there is comfort in knowing that God responds to us with power, justice, and most of all . . .

Love

The Scripture doesn't tell us that God loves, it claims that God *is* love.

Dear friends, let us practice loving each other, for love comes from God and those who are loving and kind show that they are the children of God, and that they are getting to know him better. But if a person isn't loving and kind, it shows that he doesn't know God—for God is love.

God showed how much he loved us by sending his only Son into this wicked world to bring to us eternal life through his death. In this act we see what real love is: it is not our love for God but his love for us when he sent his Son to satisfy God's anger against our sins. (1 John 4:7-10)

How could a loving God let my five-year-old brother die?

God responds to each of us out of his character of love. (It would be "out of character" for him to act any other way.) The Bible doesn't give us all the answers, but because of God's incredible love, he understands our questions.

45

Why do good people die so young? *I understand your question. I died at thirty-three.*

Why do some people have to die such painful deaths? *I understand your pain. I was beaten, whipped, and crucified.*

Even though I know he's in heaven, I miss him so much here on earth. *I understand your grief. I left heaven to come to earth.*

Why can't people just live forever and not have to die? *I understand the problem. I came to give you eternal life.*

5

What Are Some Ways to Avoid Death?

In an underground storage site near Los Angeles, human beings are being frozen solid in giant thermos bottles! The reason: hope for eternal life.

At the instant of death, these terminally ill patients are wrapped in aluminum foil, then stored in liquid nitrogen containers. They hope that when a treatment is found for their fatal disease, they'll be defrosted and cured.

The idea of "cryogenic suspension" isn't new. In 1626 the English philosopher Francis Bacon first attempted the process by stuffing a chicken with snow. The experiment with eternal life was a disaster. Bacon caught cold and died soon afterward!

However, more recently scientists began storing fresh blood in liquid nitrogen. If first soaked in an antifreeze agent, blood cells can be stored indefinitely at -320 F.

With this success as inspiration, the first human was put into cold storage at a Los Angeles company in 1967. The cost of dying to live again is a bit frosty: starting at fifteen thousand bucks in cold cash. Plus there's a one-thousand-dollar-per-year charge for "locker rent."

Scientists are skeptical about the success of putting people on ice. Cryogenic research has not found a way to freeze the entire brain quickly enough to save vital cells. So much for living forever as an ice cube.

There are some proven ways, however, to extend your life. Former secretary of health, education, and welfare Joseph Califano, Jr., claims, "Sixty-seven percent of all disease and premature death is preventable."[1] Dr. Peter Greenwald of the National Cancer Institute claims that "80 percent of cancer cases are linked to how we live our lives," so we can avoid the deadly disease eight out of ten times.[2]

Are there any secrets to living longer?

Here's how to live longer:

- Eat your Cheerios.
- Keep off extra pounds.
- Walk, don't drive, to school/work.
- Kick some butts.
- Stay sober.
- Get married, remain faithful.
- Move to Hawaii.

Maybe I'd better explain those suggestions!

We Are What We Eat

OK, if we eat our body weight at Pizza Hut we're not going to look like a Meat Lovers' pizza. And if we simply nibble at the salad bar, we're not going to look like "Swamp Thing." But our body does need healthy food to remain healthy.

Six major nutrients act as building blocks for a healthy body:

1. Carbohydrates

These nutrients come in the form of sugar and starch and provide fuel for our bodies. Bread, cereal, spaghetti, noodles, popcorn, and rice make up this category. Whole-grain breads and cereals contain fiber, which keeps us regular and acts to prevent colon-rectal cancer. Fiber may also help reduce cholesterol—the stuff that clogs up our veins.

2. Protein

Muscles, skin, hair, blood cells, and bones are mostly protein, which we get from milk, meat, eggs, cheese, nuts, beans, peas, and other protein-rich foods.

To live longer, we must reduce the amount of red meat (which also increases cholesterol) and increase our intake of fish, chicken, and turkey. Instead of fried meat, eat boiled, broiled, or baked foods.

3. Vitamins

Vitamin A helps our vision. Vitamin B keeps our nerves, muscles, and skin in good shape. Vitamin C, along with E and beta carotene (the vegetable parent of vitamin A), is thought to protect us from those nasty "free radicals" (chapter 3) that cause us to "rust." Vitamin D helps heal wounds and broken bones. Vitamin E keeps our skin smooth and may even boost our immune system. Vegetables, fruit, and milk are good sources of many vitamins.

4. Minerals

Calcium and iron are two important nutrients. Calcium, found in milk and many vegetables, builds strong bones and teeth. Iron builds up our blood and reduces feelings of fatigue. Sources of iron include fish, chicken, turkey, lean red meat, and leafy green vegetables.

5. Water

We're about 60 percent water, so it's a very important part of our diet.

6. Fat

Despite the bad rap fat has gotten recently, it is an essential nutrient. It provides energy, carries vitamins through the body, keeps us warm in cold weather, and acts as a shock absorber for our internal organs.

However, we don't need as much fat in our diet as most of us take in. Vegetable oil and margarine are much better (and safer) sources of fat than animal fat and butter.

And most of us can get by on less fat than we pack away into storage. By maintaining our ideal weight, we lower our chances of high blood pressure and heart disease. Here's what the American Medical Association recommends. (Height is without shoes; weight is without clothes.)

We get most of our nutrients by eating the following each day:

HEIGHTS	MEN	WOMEN
4' 10"		92–119
4' 11"		94–122
5'		96–125
5' 1"		99–128
5' 2"	112–141	102–131
5' 3"	115–144	105–134
5' 4"	118–148	108–138
5' 5"	121–152	111–142
5' 6"	124–156	114–146
5' 7"	128–161	118–150
5' 8"	132–166	122–154
5' 9"	136–170	126–158
5' 10"	140–174	130–163
5' 11"	144–179	134–168
6'	148–184	138–173
6' 1"	152–189	
6' 2"	156–194	
6' 3"	160–199	
6' 4"	164–204	

- Two servings of meat, fish, or poultry.
- Three to four servings of dairy products. (Sorry, Dairy Queen Blizzards don't count!)
- One serving each of vegetable and fruit.
- Four servings of bread or cereal.

A More Youthful-looking Body

As I was sitting down in front of the TV with my bag of Oreos, this ad caught my attention.

Europe's Miracle Body Shaper
"FIGURE-TRON II"
For Those Vital Figure-toning Wonders of:
3,000 Sit-ups without Moving an Inch
10 Miles of Jogging Lying Flat on Your Back

For just $19.95 (plus $3.00 for postage and handling), the announcer promised, I could wire myself up to "Unitronic" electrodes and have "tiny micro-electronic impulses tone your muscles *five hundred times a minute!* Automatically works on slack, flabby muscles *in just fifteen minutes a day! All you do is lie there—amazing Figure-tron II tones your body's sag spots. It's like hours of exercise in just a few minutes' time!* Literally dial in a more youthful looking, more beautiful body."

And, of course, there was the model with the "youthful looking, more beautiful body"!

We all know that regular exercise will keep us younger longer, but we'd rather spend $19.95 on some gadget than actually exercise. As the Nike tennis shoe commercials advise, "Just Do It."

The American Medical Association makes the following three recommendations:[3]

1. Have, at least three times a week, an exercise period at least twenty minutes long with little or no pause for rest. Doctors recommend that we choose activities that make us feel "breathless, sweaty, and aware of our heart beating." They warn, however, not to do anything so stressful that it would make us "dizzy or nauseated, or risk straining muscles or joints." Always do warm-up and cool-down exercises before and after strenuous activity.

2. Choose enjoyable exercises that fit into your schedule.

The goal is to develop a lifelong habit of physical fitness—not just spring training to try to fit into last year's swimsuit.

3. Take your time. Our bodies don't get out of shape overnight and, unfortunately, they don't get back into shape in a day.

The following is the AMA's analysis of various exercises. The calories column shows how many units are burned in twenty minutes of that activity. The heart/lungs, flexibility, and strength columns note benefits in these areas. Like movie reviews, four stars is excellent.

Check with your doctor before beginning an exercise

ACTIVITY	CALORIES	HEART/LUNGS	FLEXIBILITY	STRENGTH
EASY WALKING	60	★	★	★
GOLF	90	★	★	★
BRISK WALKING	100	★★	★	★★
GYMNASTICS	140	★★	★★★	★★
DANCING	160	★★	★★★	★
EASY JOGGING	160	★★	★	★★
TENNIS	160	★★★	★★★	★★
DOWNHILL SKIING	160	★★★★	★★★	★★★
CROSS-COUNTRY SKIING	180	★★★★	★★★	★★★
SOCCER	180	★★★	★★★	★★★
FOOTBALL	180	★★★	★★	★★★
RACQUETBALL	200	★★★	★★★	★★
BRISK JOGGING	210	★★★★	★★	★★★
BICYCLING	220	★★★★	★★	★★★
SWIMMING	240	★★★★	★★★★	★★★★

plan if you are overweight; a smoker; or under treatment for high blood pressure, heart, lung, or kidney disease, or diabetes.

The rest of you, "Drop and give me ten!" (Push-ups, that is. Hey, it sure beats pushing up daisies.)

Up in Smoke

Want to improve your popularity at school? Want to look younger longer? Want to cut your chances of heart disease and stroke in half? Want to reduce your odds of lung cancer by 1,100 percent? Then kick some butts—cigarette butts.

According to a University of Michigan study, over 60 percent of high-school seniors view smoking as a "dirty habit." And when asked if taking a drag "looks independent and liberated," 85 percent said no. The majority felt smokers are only "trying to *look* mature."

Smoking takes a toll, not only on your social life (who wants to kiss an ashtray?), but on your face as well. Studies show that the carbon monoxide in smoke deprives your face of oxygen, increasing wrinkles and complexion problems.

Will smoking really kill you?

But that's nothing compared with what it does to your life expectancy! Smoking killed 434,000 people in the United States last year. That's more than the entire population of Chattanooga, Tennessee, and nearly the entire population of Wyoming! Smoking is the single most preventable cause of death in the United States.

What makes smoking so dangerous? Well, there are enough chemicals in burning tobacco to start your own hazardous landfill—4,027 in all. More than 200 of them are known poisons, and 16 are known to cause cancer.

Carbon monoxide (CO), found in cigarettes, is identical to car exhaust! (Your bloodstream carries CO better than O_2, so it can be deadly to put CO into your system.)

Hydrogen cyanide, used to execute criminals in gas chambers, also is found is cigarette smoke. And recent studies have shown that cigarette smoke is radioactive and can actually create "hot spots" in lungs. (The people smoking up the school bathrooms are more hazardous to your health than a nuclear power plant.)

Then there's the tar in cigarettes, which is virtually identical to the black coating on the mall parking lot. One year of smoking can produce a quart of blacktop sealant in a smoker's lungs.

Perhaps the most dangerous chemical is nicotine. This extremely addictive drug is both a stimulant and a depressant. It's one of the few drugs that has absolutely no medical benefits because it acts so unpredictably. Some claim that nicotine is more addictive than heroin or cocaine, since only one out of three who seriously try to kick the smoking habit are able to do so.

If you smoke, here are some suggestions that may work for you.

1. "Get with the program." There are many free no-smoking programs available:

"The Seven-Day Quitter's Guide"
The American Cancer Society
3340 Peachtree NE
Atlanta, GA 30326

The National Cancer Institute
1-800-4-CANCER

The American Lung Association
P.O. Box 596DN
New York, NY 10001

If self-help programs don't work, see your doctor. He or she can offer many new medical treatments and drugs (nicotine gum, nicotine patches, etc.) that can help reduce the craving for a smoke.

2. Don't buy cigarettes. Don't carry a lighter or matches. If you have to constantly bum cigarettes and lights, it maybe more difficult to continue smoking.

3. Tell your friends you're quitting, and ask for their help to keep you accountable. Spend time with friends who don't smoke.

4. When the urge to smoke hits, take a deep breath. Hold it for ten seconds, release it slowly. Taking deep, rhythmic breaths is similar to smoking, only you'll inhale clean air—not poisonous gases.

5. Get rid of smoker's breath by brushing your teeth several times. Notice how much better your mouth tastes and breath smells!

6. Cleanse your body of nicotine. Drink lots of water, fruit juices, or caffeine-free soft drinks. Coffee and caffeinated soft drinks can increase your urge to smoke.

7. Exercise to help relieve tension. (If you skipped over the section "A More Youthful-looking Body," check it out. I know, exercise is no fun, but neither is dying before forty.)

8. Eat rather than smoke—but stick to low-calorie, high-nutrition foods. Avoid spicy foods, which can trigger a desire for a smoke.

9. Change habits associated with smoking. Try to avoid the spots where you used to smoke. (Use the school restroom only when absolutely necessary!)

10. Use the money you save by not buying cigarettes to reward yourself with a new CD, new clothes, or the first book in this series—*Sex Is Not a Four-Letter Word*.

You'll also be rewarding yourself with better-looking skin and fewer wrinkles, increased energy and endurance, better and more restful sleep, fewer colds and infections, lower risk of lung cancer and heart disease, and a longer life.

None for the Road

Besides tobacco, alcohol is the most abused drug in the United States—and the most deadly. Alcohol is the number-one cause of automobile deaths; half of all those killed are teens.

Heavy drinking over a number of years can cause damage to the liver and pancreas; cause increased risk of cancer of the mouth, larynx, esophagus, and liver; and lead to malnutrition, stomach irritation, less resistance to diseases, and irreversible damage to the brain and nervous system. On the average, a heavy drinker's life is cut short by ten to twelve years!

Some believe they can avoid these problems with the following myths.

Myth #1: Beer drinkers consume less alcohol. While beer does have less alcohol than wine or liquor, beer drinkers don't drink any less alcohol. Beer (at 4 percent alcohol) is usually drunk in twelve-ounce servings, which contain *one-half ounce of alcohol.* Wine (at 12 percent alcohol) is usually drunk in four-ounce servings, which contain *one-half ounce of alcohol.* Hard liquor ("86 proof" has 43 percent alcohol) is usually drunk in one-ounce glasses, which contain—you guessed it—*one-half ounce of alcohol.*

Myth #2: Lite beers have less alcohol. They have fewer calories, but not less alcohol. Unfortunately, because they're "less filling," users may end up drinking more than usual.

Why do people drive drunk even though they know they could get killed?

Myth #3: Eating while drinking will keep a person from getting drunk. Eating does slow down the rate at which alcohol is absorbed into the bloodstream, but it doesn't prevent alcohol's effects. As a result, a person may end up drinking too much because of the delayed reaction. This is especially dangerous since someone may feel completely sober when he or she leaves a restaurant, but the alcohol may kick in with full effects on the drive home.

Myth #4: When someone gets down to serious drinking and begins to urinate at roughly the same rate as beer is being chugged, the alcohol passes right through and has little effect on the body. What is passing through the body is the excess water, not the alcohol. The alcohol is oxidized—or burned up—by the body at a steady rate of three-eighths of an ounce per hour—which means a good portion of it is left in the body!

Myth #5: Black coffee is the best way to sober up. Wrong again. And forget about cold showers, fresh air, serious talk, food, exercise, or deep breathing. Once the alcohol is in the stomach, it goes straight to the bloodstream. There is nothing that will speed up the oxidation described earlier. Black coffee—being a stimulant—will help a drunk person wake up but not "sober up." He or she is now simply a *wide-awake* drunk.

The real danger about these "remedies" is that the drinker may be convinced that he or she is sober, while the body's alcohol content has not been remedied.

If you—or a friend of yours—are having problems with alcohol (signs include missing school, getting drunk, becoming aggressive, etc.), here are some ways that you can get help for yourself or your friend.

1. Learn all you can about alcoholism. The more you know, the more you can help—and the less frustrated you'll become.

2. Don't "preach," threaten, or insult the alcoholic in an effort to get him or her to quit drinking. The person will be better motivated by love and support than by humiliation.

3. Don't "cover" for the alcoholic's behavior. As long as drinkers don't have to face up to the consequences of the things they do when drunk, there will be no motivation to

57

quit. While it may seem cruel to let a friend who has passed out spend the night in his or her own vomit on the bathroom floor, alcoholics often must suffer some pain before there's any desire to get help. (Obviously, you should help a friend who is in a life-threatening situation, such as someone who has passed out on a sidewalk on the coldest night of winter. But if it's warm weather, let your friend wake up to the fact that his or her drinking is out of control.)

4. When the person is ready to admit his or her need for help, suggest a support group such as AA (Alcoholics Anonymous). There are also groups for family members: ALATEEN for children of alcoholic parents and AL-ANON for husbands, wives, and relatives of alcoholics. All three programs are free and are available in most cities. For free information, write:

National Council on Alcoholism
2875 Northwind Drive, Suite 225
East Lansing, MI 48823

More Deadly Drugs
Caffeine

Yup. Dr. Patricia Mutch, director of the Institute for Alcoholism and Drug Dependency, claims that caffeine (found in coffee, some soft drinks, and chocolate) can be a killer. Caffeine makes the heart beat faster and stronger, increases anxiety, stimulates the stomach to secrete more acid, increases the levels of sugar and fatty acids in the blood, and causes problems with the excretory system.

And if that's not enough to make you switch to caffeine-free Coke, the good doctor continues. Caffeine "is known as a mutagenic agent; it can negatively alter genetic material. This may increase the risk of cancer." She also adds that "caffeine does not improve memory, comprehension, or the ability to function."[4]

Obviously, caffeine and coffins don't have a direct connection, but everything we can do to avoid unnecessary risks increases our chances of living longer.

Cocaine

"Coke" is one of the most widely used illegal drugs and one of the most addictive. Heavy users must increase dosages to get the same effect—and those effects can prove deadly. Cocaine can cause cold sweats, dizziness, chest pain, heart problems, vomiting, uncontrollable shaking, loss of sleep, and weight loss. The number of reported deaths, which result from multiple seizures followed by heart and lung failure, is steadily increasing.

Inhalants

I got my first lecture on drug abuse in second grade when I was building a model of a Tom Cat fighter plane. "James Norman Watkins, that airplane glue will rot your brains out if you don't open a window." It turned out Mom and Dad were absolutely right. Intentionally inhaling glue, hair spray, or gasoline can cause damage not only to the brain but also to the liver, kidneys, and bone marrow. Inhalants may produce irregular heartbeats and loss of oxygen to the brain resulting in a "high" feeling—and occasionally death.

Marijuana

While some claim pot, or grass, is a "safe" drug, research has shown opposite results. Because marijuana smokers inhale more deeply and hold the smoke in longer, their lungs are in much more danger than the lungs of regular cigarette smokers. And pot smoke contains even more cancer-causing ingredients than tobacco smoke.

PCP

Angel dust, or "super pot," is potentially deadly because it gives users the feeling that they are all-powerful and that nothing can hurt them. PCP users have jumped from tall buildings believing they could fly, have burned to death because they could feel no pain, and can become violent and destructive to others and themselves.

Steroids

Anabolic steroids—the synthetic version of the male hormone testosterone—have been used illegally to build up muscle strength in both male and female athletes and bodybuilders. (These are not to be confused with corticosteroids, which doctors legally and safely prescribe to reduce the swelling of arthritis and sports injuries.) Anabolic steroids are effective, especially for women, but they have some deadly side effects. They build up not only muscles but tumors. They can cause heart disease, liver damage, and hormonal imbalance.

Side effects in men include prostate cancer, shrinking testicles, and enlarged breasts; in women, a lower voice, more facial hair, shrinking breasts, and even baldness. Steroid use can lead to aggressiveness ("roid rage"), depression, and mental illness, including hallucinations and hearing voices.

East German athlete Birgit Dressel (twenty-six years old), New Zealand discus thrower Robin Tait (forty), and NFL football player Lyle Alzado (forty-three) all died as a direct result of steroid abuse. Because the drug is illegal, many other professional and amateur athletes are suspected to have died of steroid use, with doctors and family members keeping the cause of death secret.

Other potentially deadly drugs include amphetamines ("uppers"), barbiturates ("downers"), heroin, and LSD ("acid").

Married or Buried?

If you want to double your chances of a long life, get married. That's the conclusion of several university studies.[5]

Researchers tracked eight thousand middle-aged men in Sweden. At the end of ten years, 9 percent of the married men had died, but 20 percent of the single men had died. A similar study in Finland adjusted its results to account for tobacco use, cholesterol levels, and blood pressure—and even taking these factors into consideration, married men still outlived single men two to one.

These findings have also been verified in the United States. Robert H. Coombs of the UCLA School of Medicine has confirmed that "married people live longer and generally are more emotionally and physically healthy than the unmarried. The therapeutic benefit of marriage remains relatively unrecognized."[6]

In 1987 Debra Umberson found that not just men but women live longer married than single, and that those married with children had the best survival rates. She concludes that those with the responsibility of a spouse and children tend to avoid destructive behaviors, such as excessive drinking, drug use, risk-taking, and disorderly living.

And even when they do face life-threatening illnesses, married people have better rates of survival. A Michigan Cancer Foundation study concluded that "marriage influences survivorship among cancer patients."[7] Perhaps the support of a spouse and a desire to survive for his or her sake contribute to survival rates.

Of course, merely saying "I do" will not add years to your life. But those who are willing to make a lifelong commitment tend to live longer by avoiding destructive behaviors. There's also some real health "assurance" in remaining sexually pure before marriage and sexually faithful to your spouse.

AIDS and Aging

Most sexually transmitted diseases are more damaging than deadly: Chlamydia can cause painful urination, sterility (inability to have children), premature births, birth defects, and stillbirths. Gonorrhea, or "the clap," damages skin, bones, joints, tendons, and reproductive as well as other organs. Herpes simplex virus 2, which has no cure at this time, affects sexual organs as well as the lower body. Half of the children born to HSV-2 carriers will die; one-fourth will be brain damaged. Venereal warts are not only irritating, but babies who contract these from infected mothers can die if the warts develop in the child's throat or lungs.

At least two of the forty STDs (Sexually Transmitted Diseases) can mean RIP (Rest in Peace).

AIDS

AIDS (acquired immunodeficiency syndrome) destroys a victim's ability to fight off diseases and infections. Since his or her body has no defense against these, AIDS is 100 percent deadly. Most victims lose a lot of weight and often die of pneumonia. But AIDS can have *no* symptoms.

The AIDS virus is spread by blood-to-blood or by blood-to-semen contact, such as occurs through sexual intercourse, homosexual acts, or sharing of hypodermic needles. There is *no* proof that AIDS can be spread by other than blood-to-blood or blood-to-semen contact since the virus dies very quickly when exposed to air.

When AIDS was first observed, 73 percent of its victims were homosexual men, and 17 percent were addicts who shared dirty needles to shoot drugs. Now, 89 percent of AIDS is spread through sexual intercourse between men and women. In America, the fastest-growing group of victims is heterosexual teens and young adults. Since the virus can take up to ten years to show itself, this means that many contracted AIDS in junior high!

The predictions as to how many people have AIDS and how many will die keep changing. Some claim that 250,000 people in America have already died of AIDS. There may be as many as 100 million carriers of this deadly virus throughout the world. And many carriers don't even realize they have the disease.

Syphilis

Another deadly STD is syphilis, which lives in the warm, moist areas of the mouth, vagina, and urethra. After sexual contact (kissing or contact with sexual organs), a small, red, painless sore appears. These chancres (pronounced "shank-ers") appear on the penis or on the mouth. They may be present in the vagina or cervix of the woman, but not noticeable. In one to five weeks the chancres usually disappear.

But the disease continues to spread through the bloodstream. About six weeks after the sores disappear, the person with syphilis may have a headache, fever, loss of appetite, and a red skin rash that doesn't itch. Again, these symptoms disappear by themselves. Even without treatment, all symptoms disappear in about six months—but the disease doesn't go away.

If not caught early and effectively treated with penicillin, the disease silently spreads and years later can cause blindness, heart disease, paralysis, brain damage, or death.

Nearly 100,000 people contract syphilis in the United States each year.

Some claim that "safe sex" with condoms is the answer to the thousands of deaths caused by sexually transmitted diseases. But how safe is sex with a condom?

The American Medical Association claims that condoms fail to prevent pregnancy one out of seven times.

United States government tests claim the failure rate is more like one in five. But the failure rate for preventing sexually transmitted diseases is worse. According to the *New England Journal of Medicine,* condoms fail 30 percent of the time (or roughly one out of three times) in preventing the spread of AIDS. .

How can you keep from dying of AIDS?

"Safe sex" is about as safe as playing Russian roulette with two bullets in a six-chamber revolver! The only truly safe sex is with one partner for a lifetime.

Pacific Paradise

Where you live can also increase or decrease your life expectancy. According to the National Center for Health Statistics, Hawaiians have the longest life expectancy: 77.02 years.

In addition to Hawaii, the top-ten life expectancy list includes Minnesota (76.15), Iowa (75.81), Utah (75.81), North Dakota (75.71), Nebraska (75.49), Wisconsin (75.35), Kansas (75.31), Colorado (75.3), and Idaho (75.19).

The ten worst places to live—if you want to live a long time—are the District of Columbia (69.2), Louisiana (71.74), South Carolina (71.85), Mississippi (71.98), Georgia (72.22), Alaska (72.24), Alabama (72.53), Nevada (72.64), West Virginia (72.84), and North Carolina (72.96).

There are many factors that contribute to life expectancy in a location (crime rates, public health care, poverty level, etc.), so simply moving to Hawaii is no guarantee—but it couldn't hurt either!

PART THREE

How can a person deal with death?

*K*evin's brain seemed to be on "spin cycle" as Lori clung to him and cried. Do I just stand here with my hands in my pockets? . . . Why would anyone drink and drive? . . . Do I hold her? . . . Why the creepy organ music? . . . What is everyone thinking about us like this? . . . Who invented ties, anyway? . . . Are we holding up the funeral?

Slowly, Kevin pulled his hands out of his pockets and cautiously put his arms around Lori. Immediately she pulled away. "I'm ready to sit down," she announced with composure.

They quickly found two seats in the back row. Though Kevin's mind continued to whirl, he managed to remember enough of the minister's message to quote in his article: "a good student . . . active in Student Council . . . the hardest days are ahead as the reality that you'll never see Brian again in this life overcomes each of you . . . feelings of shock, denial, anger, confusion . . . a day that you are forced to confront your own mortality . . . you can be assured of eternal life. . . ."

As the student pallbearers carried Brian's casket to the waiting hearse outside, Kevin tried to put together what he knew intellectually—Brian is dead—*with what he felt emotionally*—This is all a bad dream; we'll all wake up tomorrow morning, and Brian will be back at his desk in Sociology class.

"Could we stop by Community Hospital and see Renee on the way back to school?" Lori interrupted his thoughts.

"Ah, sure, I don't see why not," Kevin said aloud. But inside he was pleading: Come on! Haven't we had enough emotional trauma for one day?

She looks more dead than Brian did, *Kevin thought as he gazed at Renee through the windows of the ICU. No heavy makeup or pink floodlights hid the fact that she had gone through the windshield face first. She clung to life by IV tubes, EKG wires, automatic blood pressure cuffs, and a respirator. After a moment, Mrs. Roberts noticed them and came out into the hallway.*

Lori spoke first. "Ah . . . Mrs. Roberts, I'm Lori Reed and this is Kevin Farra. We're friends of Renee's."

Seeing the woman's matted hair and smudged mascara, Kevin assumed Renee's mother hadn't left her bedside post during the past four days.

"Oh yes. You're the young people from the school paper who called about Renee." They stood in silence gazing at Renee's closed eyes, and then at the monitors, and then at the respirator, which was forcing her chest to rise and fall.

"Ah . . . do you know how the flow test came out?" Kevin finally asked after an eternal silence.

Mrs. Roberts took a deep breath. "Not good. The doctor says she's—" She stopped. Kevin held his breath in anticipation of the answer he feared was coming. "Renee's brain-dead."

Lori grabbed Kevin's hand and blurted out, "But the heart monitor . . . her heart's beating and she's breathing."

"I know. But the doctor says that the machines are doing all that," Mrs. Roberts answered as she wiped her eyes with the back of her hand. "When my husband gets here . . ." She paused again as if trying to understand her own words. "They're going to turn off the machines."

Kevin's hand felt numb as Lori squeezed harder. "I'm really sorry, Mrs. Roberts," Lori sobbed.

"Ah . . . we, ah . . . probably ought to be going," Kevin suggested. His heart and head were pounding in unison.

As they drove across town, Kevin and Lori sat in silence until they pulled into the school parking lot. Kevin turned off the car, but neither made a move to get out.

Kevin was trying to figure out what was happening between them. Why did she grab hold of me at the funeral home and then pull away when I put my arms around her? Why did she grab my hand when we were visiting Renee? Was it just all the emotion of the funeral and death and everything? Or is there something—

"Thanks for being there for me, Kevin." Lori's voice broke into his thoughts. "You've always seemed to be there. Remember when I broke my ankle sliding into third base? You sacrificed your Sno-Kone to ice it down." She paused and looked into Kevin's eyes. "You're a good friend."

With that Lori bounded out of the car and headed toward the line of yellow school busses. He watched her get on bus number five, hoping to see her wave good-bye, but she just took a seat and stared straight ahead. Women, *he thought as he started his car to drive home.* Who can understand them?

6

How Can a Person Deal with Accidents and Terminal Illnesses?

How can a person deal with death? I'd like to introduce you to six friends who stare into the chalky face of death on a daily basis.

Ron Sloan is a medical doctor specializing in family practice. During his career, he's held dead babies in his arms, told teens that they have leukemia, and performed CPR on patients who never revived. Tina Bowen and Charlene Baungartner are registered nurses who specialize in intensive care and emergency room nursing. We'll meet these three people in just a few moments.

In the next chapter I'll introduce you to Jerry Custer, captain of a small-town police department, who's personally dealt with three murders, four attempted murders, and seventeen suicides. He says he's lost count of the fatal auto accidents he's investigated.

In chapters 9 and 10 we'll meet Jim and Mike Stone, funeral directors, as we observe the embalming of a body and talk about funerals of teens.

Monitoring Death

Tina and Charlene spend most of their eight-hour shift watching oscilloscope screens that monitor the heart rates of six patients who are more or less close to death. Electrical sensors are glued to a patient's chest and sides and pick up the heart's contractions and relaxations, which then appear on a TV monitor.

Suddenly the yellow warning light flashes, and an alarm sounds on monitor four as a printer wildly pens closely spaced peaks and valleys.

Tina calmly picks up the phone and calls the nurses' station. "Hi, this is Tina. What is Mr. Trombley doing? We've got a strange pattern."

Tina waits while a nurse checks on the patient, and Charlene explains the pattern. "It's not a heart pattern. It could be a seizure, but it's more likely not. But something's going on with a lot of muscle action."

Charlene pulls off the narrow strip of paper and studies it. "I'm guessing he's brushing his teeth. See, you can see the consistent up-and-down motion that the heart monitor is picking up."

Tina continues to wait patiently for an answer. "OK, that was one of our choices—that or a seizure," she says, laughing as she hangs up the phone. "Yep, he was brushing his teeth. This happens every mealtime—all the alarms go off, and it's everybody brushing their teeth."

I'm amazed at how casually Tina and Charlene react to abnormal rhythms on the monitors.

"You learn not to make assumptions," Tina explains, "and you learn that most of the time the alarms are for harmless body movement or perhaps a wire to the sensors has come loose. For instance, a flat line that shows no rhythm—like you see on TV—rarely means a patient is dying. It usually means that there's an electrical problem with the machine, an electrode has come loose, the conducting gel that holds the sensors on the patient has dried out, or—if the patient is obese—we're not getting a good reading.

"That's why we keep the in-room monitors turned

away from the patient and family. Watching it just makes them nervous, and they start misinterpreting bodily movements for heart rhythms. They think, *Oh my God, I'm dying!* when an electrode comes loose."

But Tina and Charlene are ready for any real emergency. Each room in the intensive care unit is filled with high-tech equipment: automatic blood pressure monitors, electrocardiogram (EKG) and respiration (breathing) monitors, oxygen tubing, suction pumps for lungs, stomachs, and body cavities to keep fluids from building up, IV (intravenous) pumps that can give continuous low doses of medications directly into a vein, a call button to summon a nurse, a code blue (emergency) button, and of course—a cable TV remote.

Taped to the wall are various-sized airways (tubes which are inserted into the throat to deliver oxygen) and bite sticks, which are put in patients' mouths during a seizure to keep them from biting their tongues.

Each room's supply cupboard contains disposable gloves, goggles, masks, gowns, and aprons. "We're really cautious about body fluids," Tina explains, "especially now with the danger of AIDS and hepatitis B."

In the nurses' station, a "crash cart" sits poised for a code blue—the code indicating a stoppage of breathing and heartbeat. On top of the bright red tool chest on wheels sit the "defibrillators."

"When patients go into 'V-fib' the heart just fibrillates, or quivers, rather than beating. These paddles send an electrical shock through the heart and hopefully restores the heartbeat. We have to test it each shift to make sure it's working right." *Do doctors and nurses get used to death?*

The crash cart drawers contain medications, IV tubes in all sizes (from infant to adult), and a manual suction pump. "The pump is pretty neat, but I've never had to use it, thank God," Tina comments. Both nurses seem to be relieved at the end of their eight-hour shift that they haven't had to use any of the equipment.

While Tina claims that "death is a natural part of life," medical staff, like the rest of us, want to avoid it.

Charlene comments, "There used to be an old superstition in nursing that if you tied a knot in the patient's sheet they wouldn't die on your shift. So if you see a nurse tie a knot in your sheet—it's not good!" Everyone laughs.

What goes through a person's mind who is dying?

Denial

Elisabeth Kubler-Ross, the author of *On Death and Dying*,[1] believes that the terminally ill—and their families and friends—pass through five stages in dealing with death: denial, anger, bargaining, depression, and acceptance.

Not everyone agrees with the order of phases, and some believe people may repeat some phases, but most agree that these five feelings are always experienced by the patient, family and friends, and the medical staff.

"Denial is something we physicians have to guard against," Ron Sloan, M.D., notes over breakfast in the hospital cafeteria. "For instance, when I'm examining a pre-born's size or heart tones, I may discover something that's not quite right. There's a tendency to say to myself, *Everything is going to be OK.* And denial isn't bad. It keeps me going through the day as I have twenty more patients to see. I don't have the emotional energy to worry about the death of a pre-born. I put it out of my mind while I'm waiting for further test results. If I started the grieving process every time I was highly suspicious, I'd do a lot of unnecessary grieving."

Tina agrees. "Professionally, you almost cut yourself off.

That sounds really calloused, but you do care. You're concerned, but then again, you can't allow yourself to feel the pain. If you get into the grieving mode, you lose your professional effectiveness. Working in the ER [emergency room] in suburban Chicago was really difficult. There was no chaplain, and so if a multiple-injury accident came in and the doctors were busy, I was the one who had to tell the family."

Dr. Sloan adds, "You have to tell people gradually to help them through the denial stage. I might say, 'You have a mass in your lung that I'm concerned about. It may be nothing, but it could be something serious.' I plant the idea that this could be a major problem, but I always give hope.

"Then a short time later, with testing results, I'll say, 'This looks like it could be cancer,' but I don't say, 'You're dying.' Maybe after four meetings and additional testing I gradually give them more information. 'This could be a terminal problem.' By then, many, many times they already know it. They'll say, 'I was afraid it would be' or, 'I kinda expected it.'"

In the case of a sudden death, Dr. Sloan, like most doctors, slowly reveals the facts rather than hitting them all at once.

"Often I'm in the process of trying to revive the patient with CPR," Ron continues. "I go out to the family as soon as I can and let them know the status because they're going crazy wondering what's going on. I say something like, 'We're doing everything we can, but it doesn't look good.'

Why don't people want to talk about death?

"I may continue CPR for four or five minutes—even though I know there's no chance for survival—to give the family that time for the possibility of death to sink in. I try to give the family at least some warning before I have to tell them their loved one has died."

In the case of terminal illnesses, the denial process can be lengthy.

"The dying patient doesn't talk about his death because he doesn't want to put stress on the family. And his family doesn't talk about it because they don't want to create trauma for the patient," Ron explains.

"So my job is to try to break that major communication barrier and get them expressing their feelings. One of the ways I do that is to let the family see me talking to patients about their impending death. 'How do you feel? Any fears?' Frequently they feel relieved to talk about it. They know they're dying, so I make it legal to talk about.

"And when the family really starts talking and sharing with each other, there's a real bonding and healing. And everyone realizes how valuable they are to each other."

Tina adds, "I have a hard time with families and patients who keep from each other that a death is coming. Both need to know. If they don't, it deprives them from comforting each other. And they know deep down that death is near. I think God gives them a sixth sense."

According to Mary Fran Hazinki's *Nursing Care for the Critically Ill Child,* teens, however, have a difficult time accepting the reality of dying:

> They can understand the fact that death is permanent and that it will happen to everyone one day, however . . . they fantasize that death may be defied. Adolescents may be unable to totally accept the final reality of death because of belief in their own invincibility.
>
> Because remnants of magical thinking still persist during adolescence, teenagers may view fatal illness as a punishment or may feel guilty. Reassurance and open discussion of feelings, concerns, and fears are extremely important. Adolescents have a great deal of difficulty coping with the idea of their own death at a time when they are striving to establish their

own identity and make plans for the future. It is very difficult to face the fact they may have no future.[2]

Elisabeth Kubler-Ross suggests that adolescents shouldn't be told they are dying, but rather that they are "seriously ill."

> When they are ready to bring up the issue of death and dying, we should answer them; we should listen to them; we should hear the questions, but do not go around telling [teen] patients they are dying and deprive them of a glimpse of hope they may need in order to *live* until they die.[3]

Others disagree, pointing out that the patient knows already—either instinctively or due to the increase of medical attention, the way people act toward him or her, or the tears or awkwardness of visitors.

Regardless, the denial stage is important. It not only helps the medical staff to carry on with its other responsibilities, but it gives the patient some emotional insulation to make plans and contact family and friends.

Do you know when you're dying? How do you know?

Anger

Another phase Kubler-Ross describes is anger.

Anger at the medical staff: "Why didn't they detect it earlier?" "Why isn't the medicine working?" "Why wasn't the operation a success?"

Anger at God: "Why did you allow me to get this disease?" "Why won't—or don't—you heal me?" One thing my wife, as a minister, does is tell people it's OK to be angry with God. The psalmists seemed to be angry with

God most of the time: "Why don't you do something?" (See chapter 4 for more about this.)

This intense anger can spill over onto family and friends. Lynn Caine in her book *Widow* talks about the "craziness" of blaming her husband for dying. How dare he die and cop out on his responsibilities to her and their children!

Anger is a normal emotion as we deal with our own death or the death of a loved one. Realize that the patient is losing every earthly thing. He or she has a right to be angry, so allow it to be expressed—and don't take it personally.

Guilt

Dr. Sloan would add guilt to the list of phases. "I see this especially in expectant mothers who lose a baby due to miscarriage or stillbirth. There is a tremendous sense of guilt that they somehow caused it—even when it was no fault of their own."

Children may feel that somehow they contributed to their parents' death. Although this is usually not the case, the feelings are very real.

There is also a temptation for medical personnel to feel guilty over *what ifs*. Dr. Sloan continues, "I look back over the charts to see if I missed anything. The vast majority of the time, if you do find something you missed or could have done differently, it wouldn't have made any difference in the outcome."

Bargaining

Family members may pray, *God, if you'll let my grandmother live, I'll go to church more often. I'll even put more in the offering plate. And here's an offer you can't refuse: How 'bout if I become a missionary? You name it, I'll do it.*

The patient may pray, *God, just let me make it through the holidays.*

But God rarely responds to this version of "Let's Make a Deal." It's not that he doesn't care about our hurts and fears. It's just that he knows the best thing he can do is go through life's difficulties with us, not—*poof!*—make all our problems go away.

Depression

It is depressing to think about one's losses such as health and mobility. In a hospital bed—tethered to an IV pole—one can't play basketball, go out for pizza, swim, walk in the park, or do thousands of things he or she once enjoyed. The realization creeps in that there will be many more things that will be missed: graduating from high school, going to college, getting married, having children—the list continues to grow in one's mind.

Kubler-Ross refers to this as "preparatory grief." The patient and family begin to mourn the loss even before the death.

In chapter 8, we will talk at length about depression and its symptoms. You may want to refer to this chapter for more about this emotion that is a normal part of the dying process.

Although depressed people are depressing to be around, they need our love and company. J. Kerby Anderson, in his excellent book *Life, Death & Beyond,* writes,

When a patient is expressing himself on an emotional level, he does not need logical arguments. He needs compassion and assurance on the emotional level. Conversely, when he is seeking advice about his personal affairs, he does not need emotional statements like 'Don't worry, everything will be all right.' He needs helpful advice about finances or other affairs.[4]

Acceptance

Dying patients often come to a point of accepting their impending death with courage and a real lack of fear. They have worked through the denial, anger, bargaining, and depression—often through counseling and support groups. (Organizations such as the American Cancer Society and the Muscular Dystrophy Association sponsor such groups through their local agencies.)

"Once they reach the acceptance stage," Tina, our nurse friend, explains, "patients often beg their families to let them go, but the families put them on full code [order them revived after each heart stoppage]. One patient kept begging her family, 'Don't do this to me. Don't torture me. Let me go!' The family made the doctors and nurses do everything possible to prolong her inevitable death."

Is it scary to know that you're dying?

At this point, the life-and-death questions of "living wills," "death with dignity," and euthanasia (mercy killing) confront the doctors, hospital staff, patients, and families. And the actual definition of death continues to change. A few hundred years ago "lack of breathing" was the evidence of death. This century began by adding "lack of heartbeat" to the criteria. Now "lack of brain-wave activity" is a necessary proof.

"Right now the lines are really blurred between passive and active euthanasia. [Passive euthanasia is *allowing* the patient to die without using extraordinary measures; active euthanasia is deliberately *causing* the patient to die with a lethal injection or some other means.]

"For instance, we had a man with chronic lung disease who was literally fighting for air for three days. His heart had stopped several times, and each time he had been revived.

"Finally, he was so air hungry that his physician said, 'We can give you some morphine. It will make you feel better, but it also may cause you to go.' The patient was ready, the family was ready. So he chose morphine, and it wasn't more than twenty minutes and he was gone.

"I'm not sure if that was mercy killing or not. It wasn't a lethal dosage—it was the normal dose for pain control—but it caused him to relax and stop fighting for air. I'm just glad I wasn't the one giving the injection."

Dr. Sloan continues, "Part of my practice is helping people die, as well as helping people live. I don't put people on medicine I know won't help them. I don't put people on ventilators who aren't going to be helped by them.

"I could make an argument for lethal injection. And I can think of cases where **Is it OK to** it would have been kinder to cut a patient's last days short by a week. I think I could **pull the** even do it without any problem or real conflict, *except*—"His voice raised in vol-**plug on** ume to emphasize the word *except*. "That starts us down a slippery slope that has no **someone** ending. Society has slidden down that **who's going** slope with abortions. People now kill millions of unborns that society considers **to die** unplanned, an inconvenience, or a burden **anyway?** on society. With the rising cost of health care, society is not too far from deciding that the sick and elderly are also a burden on society."

The Netherlands have already "slidden down that slope" with an estimated five thousand Dutch citizens dying each year with doctors' assistance.[5]

America may not be far behind. Marcia Angell, the executive editor of the *New England Journal of Medicine,* says, "I think perhaps we're ready to consider euthanasia that is very, very strictly controlled."[6]

Dr. Daniel Callahan, one of America's leading bioethicists, writes that upon reaching a certain age, the elderly "have no right to burden the public purse." Callahan has suggested that those over eighty to eighty-five be cut off from the "right" to medical care.[7]

Dr. Jack Kevorkian, better known as "Dr. Death," has already been charged and declared not guilty of breaking any Michigan laws in helping several patients take their own lives with his so-called suicide machine. At least one patient, although in pain, was *not* terminally ill.

Although there are many factors to be considered in the care of truly terminal patients, both Ron and Tina agree that "when in doubt, choose life."[8]

"With the terminally ill," Ron adds, "I tell them I can't make this go away, but there are two things I can do: I can help keep your pain under control, and I can make sure you're ready to meet God. You can have the peace of knowing that if you die in a month or six months from now, that you will go to heaven. And that's consolation for you and your family."

Death

Charlene, Tina, and Ron all agree there is a "look" of death.

"There's a certain color of the skin," Ron notes. "A pale, whitish blue, gray around the mouth. There's also fluid buildup in the skin—not in the vessels, but in the tissue—that's a clue that death is near."

What's it like when you're on the edge of dying?

Tina adds, "Skin temperature is a clue, too. That's why we always check their legs and toes. If they're cold it means a lack of circulation. The body tries to conserve, and so it starts shutting down what it doesn't absolutely need—such as fingers and toes—to conserve blood for the heart and lungs. The fingers and toes feel cold, then turn purple and blue with a honeycomb pattern—blue circles with white in the middle—and then turn completely white. At the very end the skin gets clammy and then goes beyond clammy to almost waxlike."

The pulse becomes weaker. The heart rate begins to drop down below what's normal for the patient. Blood pressure decreases. Breathing becomes more shallow. And then the lungs begin filling with fluid.

Tina points to one of the monitors. "This patient's QRS's [the spaces between beats] are getting wider, and the peaks are also getting wider. That usually means death is near."

"The patients also become less responsive since there is a loss of blood supply to the brain," Ron adds.

Can you know for sure if somebody's dying?

"You can pretty well bet," Tina continues, "if they tell you they're going to die, they probably will. Others will say 'I don't think I'm going to make it through the night' or 'I'm prepared. I'm going to meet God.' They have a sense that death is near—unless it's a sudden death like an accident or sudden stroke."

Charlene has the reputation of being the one on whose shift people die. "A lot of nurses pray, 'God, don't let 'em die on my shift,' but I let them. When they say, 'I'm gonna die,' I don't say, 'You gotta hang in there.' I just hold their hand and say, 'That's OK, I'm here for you. Your family's here for you'—even though most of the family are huddled together in the far corner of the room. Some of the patients are alert to the last minute, and some are unconscious and look like their soul left two days ago and their body hasn't caught up."

Ron admits, "There's one thing I've learned about working with death, you can't accurately anticipate it. You can have people with all the symptoms mentioned, and they'll walk out of the hospital a week later. You can have a cancer patient that you expect to live less than six months, and six years later you're still doing their annual examinations. Or, worse, you can tell someone they're perfectly healthy, and a few days later they're faceup in a flower bed from a fatal heart attack.

"So I tell 'terminal' patients, 'You have information that says you're going to die. Perhaps your time period is a little more defined than everybody else's. But you're still in the same situation the rest of us are in. I may well beat you to the grave by walking out the door and getting nailed. So it's important to always be ready for death.'" (We'll talk about preparing for death in chapter 12.)

Relief

Dr. Sloan would also add relief to the list of phases. "In a terminal illness, there is a tremendous emotional and financial burden for the family and friends. And when the patient dies, there is a sense of relief: 'We can get on with our life.'"

Many survivors feel guilty for feeling relief, but this emotional release is healthy and in no way detracts from the value of or love they had for the dying person.

Although Charlene, Tina, and Ron have witnessed hundreds of deaths, they admit they still feel the pain.

"If I've been close to the person—personally or have been with them professionally for years—I feel the same pain that everyone else does," Ron admits. "And even if there has been very little involvement, it still takes a toll on me like everybody else." (We'll talk about the after-death grieving process in chapter 11.)

7

How Can a Person Deal with Murder?

Death surrounds the small dispatch room at the Garrett Police and Fire Department.

FBI "Wanted" notices warn of fugitives "armed with automatic weapons, including silencer-equipped machine guns," who should be considered "heavily armed and dangerous." Angry-looking men with shaggy hair and three-day-old beards glare out from the mug shots.

Beside them, two junior-high students—Jacob, thirteen, and Jaycee, twelve—smile from their posters. But the well-moussed hair and good looks hide the fact that they have been victims of "stranger abductions." A twenty-thousand-dollar reward is offered for the safe return of Jacob.

On the office TV, "Good Morning America" covers the electric-chair death of convicted rapist and murderer Roger Keith Coleman. Coleman, in a taped statement, denies that he raped, stabbed, and nearly beheaded his sister-in-law.

The dispatcher sits surrounded by computers, ashtrays, printers, Styrofoam cups of coffee, two-way radios, red telephones, and, of course, the official snack food of law enforcement—a bag of Dunkin' Donuts.

"Custer just pulled up at the side door," the dispatcher announces. "You can meet him there."

As I open the door of the blue Chevy Capri squad car and get in, the first thing I notice is a 12-gauge shotgun locked upright between Capt. Jerry Custer and myself.

The middle-aged man with a mustache wastes no time on chitchat. "So what do you want to know? Just tell me, and I'll give you an honest answer. It may not be the answer you want to hear, but I'll give it to you straight."

In less time than it takes the supercharged V-8 engine to pull out of the alley, Jerry has told me that Garrett has a population of sixty-five hundred and that in his twenty-one years on the force he's personally investigated three murders, four attempted murders, seventeen suicides, and too many traffic fatalities to count.

His words shoot out of his mouth with the rapid-fire speed of the Glock .45 automatic strapped to his waist. "It's the meanest, most effective gun in the world. I use hollow-tipped bullets. They're really safer than smaller caliber bullets that can continue through a wall of an apartment building." He pulls the thirteen-round clip out of the gun to show me the bullets. "These things flatten out and stay in whatever you hit. They've got terrific stopping power."

As he steers with one hand and reholsters his weapon with the other, I have a second to ask a question.

"Any memorable homicides that stand out?"

"Yeah. We're one block from the scene." This time his voice is soft and subdued. He pulls the cruiser up to a run-down gray duplex with gaudy green trim. The porch roof is sagging, and one window is boarded up. He now talks slowly and deliberately.

"In 1978 we had the disappearance of a ten-year-old girl named Kaci.* She was last seen alive here—had been shoveling snow to make some money to buy a gift for her aunt, who had just had a baby."

His voice quivers, then regains its authoritative tone. "I

*(not her real name)

started praying. In fact, I called my church and told them to start the telephone prayer chain for this little girl. She was in my son's class at school, so I really took it personally." He pauses again. "Because it was winter, we didn't wait the normal twenty-four hours but got out the dispatch to all the area police departments and news agencies within twelve hours.

"A couple days later I got a call from the Fort Wayne Fire Department. They had found her hat—a Chessie railroad hat that could only be purchased in Ohio—and her snowmobile boot that also was kinda unique. Soon after that we found her body jammed under a log in Cedar Creek.

"A guy in his thirties had invited her into his apartment and given her some alcohol and some joints. After she had passed out, he stuffed her leotard down her throat and then—he was a necrophiliac, a guy who has sex with dead bodies—after he had killed her, he raped her.

"I felt like a big old sheepdog where a wolf had gotten in and got one of the lambs. I felt responsible. There were several times in the investigation that I just went into my office, closed the door, and just cried. I just felt so helpless.

"The [expletive] only got seven to fourteen years!" His voice rises, and he grips the steering wheel tighter. "I was so [expletive for *angry*] after the trial that I went over to the home of one of the state investigators who had worked the case. We just drank and cried and hugged each other and wondered if there wasn't something we could have done.

"I'm not a 'good cop' because I show my emotions. I let stuff get to me—and you just can't, I guess. So sometimes you try to sluff it off with humor.

"One time I was asked by a woman to come to her house and take the high-powered rifles and compound hunting bows away from her husband, who had just gotten out of a mental hospital. I thought, *Great. I get shot with a bow and arrow, and the paper's going to have fun with 'Custer's Last Stand.'*

"It's not that we joke because we're insensitive—it's just

that dark humor helps you keep your sanity sometimes. But a lot of times that doesn't even work. For instance . . ."

He pulls into a nice residential section of town with cedar-sided apartments in a grove of pine trees.

"David*—he was fifteen—lived in apartment 10. He was a good kid, good baseball player, a hero to a lot of kids. But he got into drugs and dropped out of school. His sister came home from school, and there he was, hanging between the living room and dining room.

"My first thought when I got to the scene wasn't, *Is he going to heaven or hell?* It was, *What a waste!* Here's a healthy kid who just took his life, when other people, like my dad, were fighting to stay alive with cancer. It just makes me angry."

Jerry pulls out of the apartment parking lot and drives one block to a white-sided house with attached garage.

"David's best friend, Matt*—he was sixteen at the time—lived here. Matt was a National Honor Society member, and just eight months later, he shot himself through the heart.

"And then just a few months after that, his mom killed herself with carbon monoxide in the garage." We ride in silence for several blocks.

Why do people kill other people?

"What are some of the reasons that people kill others or themselves?" I ask.

"A lot of the time on reports, we just put down 'personal gain.' That can mean a lot of things: love, lust, revenge. One guy hired a hit man to kill his wife so he wouldn't have to pay alimony after a divorce. The suspect was planning to torch his house to pay the hit man. Fortunately, the 'hit man' was an Indianapolis undercover officer.

"All the violent crimes I've investigated—all of 'em—have been drug related: drugs and alcohol. I see a lot of kids smoking pot, dropping out of school, can't get a job—they

*(not his real name)

get stoned and blow their heads off. One guy who lived there," he says, pointing to a duplex, "was a mental patient who stopped taking his medicine, got suicidal, and put a shotgun under his chin. He blew the whole front of his head off. So even that's 'drug related.'

"I'm seeing a lot of what I call 'pagan-related' crimes. The media likes to call them 'satanic,' but a lot of them are just impressionable kids looking for meaning in life. I talked to one kid who had a little altar with wax skulls in his bedroom, and he was having this little ceremony and writing the Lord's Prayer backwards. He said, 'I've gotta have something to believe in.'

"Remember David, the kid who hanged himself? On the kitchen table—right by his body—was a book on numerology, a book on astrology, and a Bible opened to the Twenty-third Psalm. There was also a book called the *Necronomicon*—it's a book of spells that's more popular now that Anton LaVey's *Satanic Bible*. In his bedroom there were also chicken bones and a Ouija board.

"I've also worked attempted suicides where Dungeons and Dragons played a role in the attempt. A lot of people tell me, 'It's just a game like Monopoly,' but I've never worked any cases where kids attempted suicide playing Monopoly. D and D creates a real fascination with death—and it's dangerous for impressionable young kids.

"And there are some crimes that definitely have 'satanic slaying' clues. There's a gag order on the latest one."

Before the judge ordered all those involved in the case to keep silent, the local newspapers had printed the grisly details of the killing near Garrett. According to the girlfriend of one of the suspects:

Anthony Ault was tied to the floor of a barn . . . in Dekalb County. A cross was cut into Ault's body, and his neck was slit from ear to ear. When Ault stopped making gurgling noises, his head and hands were cut off and burned in a fire.[1]

Even though one of the suspects claims to have been a high priest in a satanic church in Indianapolis, Captain Custer won't call it a ritualistic killing.

"I can tell you this much—the victim knew too much about some other murders, so the motive wasn't necessarily a sacrifice to Satan."

"So how do you cope with all these deaths?" I ask.

"There are a lot of times that I'm just driving around and I talk to the Lord. I don't know how I make it some days, but I believe God doesn't give you more than you can handle. I don't wear armor [a bullet-proof vest] all the time—a lot of officers do—but my armor's God. Don't get me wrong, if I know I'm going into a hot situation, I'll put it on. But I've never, ever been real fearful in my job."

"Any close calls?"

"Yeah, right over there." (It seems Custer has a crime story for every block of the small town.) "I got called out to a domestic dispute—a guy beating his live-in girlfriend. I pulled up in the squad car to talk with the girlfriend. As we talked on the front porch, I caught movement out of the corner of my eye. The boyfriend had a shotgun aimed out the window and leveled right at me.

"All I could do was try to talk him into surrendering the weapon. He had the drop on me, and if I went for my gun, I'd be dead. I finally convinced him that killing me wasn't worth the electric chair, and he dropped the gun.

"Another time I was called to a barroom brawl. I prayed, *God, I'm all alone, and I don't have any backup. Lord, let me know what to do in this situation.* When I came through the door, tables and chairs were tossed around and broken bottles all over. I noticed that the one causing all the trouble was a 'good old boy' from down south. It was like God helped me understand that, like most southern boys, he probably had a lot of respect for his momma—even if he didn't for me.

"So I walked right up to him and whispered to him, 'I wanna tell you, if I have any trouble with you, I'm gonna tell your momma.' He just walked right out of the bar with me and got in the squad car. People in the bar thought I had some kind of pressure hold on him.

"So I really feel God's help in this work. And I guess it just comes down to doing what you think you ought to be doing. I really feel that I'm one of God's servants to the Garrett area."

8

How Can a Person Deal with Suicide?

I can't do anything with my hair!" Terri's mother heard her sixteen-year-old daughter complain one Monday morning.

"Maybe you could get a perm over spring break, honey. Dad's already left for work and I'm running late, so have a good day at school," Judy called as she gave her daughter a quick kiss on the cheek and hurried from the house. "Oh, your lunch money is on the kitchen counter."

When Judy returned home that afternoon at five, Terri's school bag and lunch money were still on the counter. Before she had time to wonder where her daughter was, the phone rang.

"Hi, Mrs. Davis. This is Steve. Is Terri there?"

"No, maybe she's out running. It's such a beautiful spring day." But a quick glance around the family room revealed that Terri's running shoes were exactly where she had kicked them off the night before.

"Oh, I was just wondering since she wasn't in school today."

Judy's heart began to pound as she hung up the phone and rushed to her daughter's room. Her nightshirt was tossed on the bed, but the clothes she had picked out for school were there too.

"Charlie," Judy nearly shouted to her husband on the phone. "Terri's missing!"

Charlie, too, began to panic. "It's not like Terri to not leave a note if she's going to be gone."

When Charlie pulled into the driveway, he noticed that their third car, "The Bomb," was also missing.

As Charlie walked toward the front door, he glanced through the garage window and saw "The Bomb" with all the dash lights lit up.

Judy noticed Charlie's frightened expression. "Stay here, Judy. I think I found Terri."

How many teens commit suicide each year?

As he opened the garage door, Charlie was nearly overcome by the exhaust fumes. There in the backseat, slumped over, was Terri.

Charlie pounded on the top of the car and screamed, "Oh my God, no! No!"

"When I touched her, she was cold and hard. I knew she had been dead for a long time," her father recalls as we sit talking with a tape recorder and a plate of chocolate chip cookies between us.

"This is a picture of Terri." Charlie proudly, tenderly takes an eight-by-ten photo down from the wall. Judy and Charlie Davis speak about the suicide of their daughter with determined, controlled emotions. During the five years since Terri's death, they have spoken at numerous high schools—including Terri's own school—about the growing problem of teen suicide.

More than five thousand young people between fifteen and twenty-four kill themselves each year. That same number *attempt* suicide every *day*.

Down Times Are Normal

Judy takes a sip of coffee and a deep breath. "We just thought Terri was going through the normal ups and downs that a typical teen goes through."

Charlie agrees. "Looking back we can see the symptoms of depression, but at the time—and even now—it didn't seem to be more than the normal stress of adolescence."

In my book *Sex Is Not a Four-Letter Word,* I spend seven chapters assuring teens that adolescent changes are normal, healthy, and temporary. So times of depression are a part of that hormone-driven roller coaster.

What's the most common reason for suicide?

Even saints like Moses, Elijah, and Jonah went through periods of extreme depression and, yes, suicidal thoughts! (Check out Numbers 11:10-15; 1 Kings 19:1-5; and Jonah 4:9.)

But keep in mind that:

Down Times Are Temporary

Judy warns teens, "Death is so final. If you take your life, you'll never go to your junior-senior prom; you're never going to go to college; you're never going to see your friends get married. That's it. There's no coming back. So I tell students, try to make it through the next week, or the next day, or even the next hour."

If you're thinking about suicide, consider this: *Suicide is a permanent solution to a temporary problem.*

No matter how bad you feel now, it's probably only temporary. Most down times last only a few hours or days. A very few last a month or more. So be encouraged that with some outside help, feelings of depression don't have to be permanent.

You will, without a doubt, have high days and low days in your life. But mostly there will be ordinary days—you know—the ones where you just go through the motions of school, home, or church. They're not bad days, but they're nothing to write your pen pal about.

It's interesting that the days we experience often follow

a pattern. People seldom have only low days or only ordinary days. We experience them all, at varying times, for various lengths of time. Our moods can be triggered by all kinds of things: a girl's monthly cycle, sickness, high and low air pressure, the season of the year, or even eating pepperoni pizza before bed.

There are certain times of year when suicides are more common. November seems to have the most suicides of any month. It looks depressing when days are growing colder and nights are growing longer. Upcoming holidays often emphasize family problems or breakups (you won't be together or you won't be looking for a present for the special person this year).

What's a reason not to commit suicide?

There are "low days" on the calendar. Most suicides occur on Monday. And there are other times when we are prone to depression: the week before school finals, term paper deadlines, the last or first day of classes (depending if you love or hate school). February 14 can be low if you don't have a Valentine or a date for the big school party. Anniversaries of a loss or tragedy can bring low days back each year, often in living color and stereo sound.

But a thirteen-year-old girl provided this note of hope on her survey:

> **Death is not something to fear, but it's not an easy way out of life's problems either. We should strive to overcome our problems, then we become better people in the end.**
> **There is hope.**

Down Times Can Be Overcome

The prophet Isaiah had some down times, too. He wrote:

[God] gives strength to the weary and increases the power of the weak. Even youths grow tired and weary, and young men stumble and fall; but those who hope in the Lord will renew their strength. They will soar on wings like eagles; they will run and not grow weary, they will walk and not be faint. (Isaiah 40:29–31, NIV)

Down times (even occasional thoughts of checking out for good) are normal ingredients in life. It may take some time to get over the feelings of hurt and disappointment, and that's tough because we live in an "instant" society: instant drinks, microwave popcorn, and fast food. Sometimes we think our emotional state should change in thirty seconds or less.

"Just add a little alcohol or drugs to taste," our friends may suggest. Even some churches offer instant recipes: "Just pray about it and all your problems will instantly disappear." But none of these instant cures work.

It's true that the only one who can help us endure and overcome bad times is God. He *is* powerful and able. Be he isn't a vending machine or a magic wand that will just make it all better. He is there to go through our low times with us, not to make the low times disappear. He is the one who can lead us, through human as well as spiritual help.

Physical Rest

The cure for down times or depression may be as simple as getting caught up on sleep! Here's part of a letter from a teen named Brad:

Last year I was really hopping to keep up. I had a full schedule of accelerated courses, I was in the choir, in the school play, had a paper route, was the youth treasurer, and trying to keep honor-roll grades.

About January, I was physically and emotionally wiped out. I couldn't care less about anything. I just sat there like a zombie. I felt nothing. I gave nothing. I was getting depressed.

I finally told our youth sponsor about my schedule; she said I probably didn't need to go to a doctor or the minister. I just needed to go to bed.

Anyway, to make a long story short, I got out of several of those things and began to get more sleep each night. What a difference!

In a month's time, I bounced back and was full of joy that I hadn't felt for so long a time.

Spiritual Restoration

Sometimes what we call depression is actually the emptiness we feel when God is left out of our lives. (You may want to skip ahead to chapter 21, "I Don't Have a Question," to read how God wants to help in this area of your life. You may be amazed what a difference it will make!)

And remember, there is nothing—absolutely nothing—that you have done that God won't forgive if you ask him.

Sixteen-year-old Matt*—forgot that—and shot himself. Here are the actual letters he wrote to his high school and to his brother:

> PLEASE READ THE FOLLOWING TO THE
> HIGH SCHOOL KIDS!!
> Now everything is a big joke. Parties, Drugs, Booze and fun. Well stop and look where you are going. I laughed at the warnings too and now look where I'm at. Dead!!! You that heard me preach saw how God

*(not his real name)

changed my life. He can change yours too!! When he does, you better not turn back. Discipline yourselves now!! Draw near to God through Jesus Christ now!!! If you don't begin practicing obedience and self-discipline now, you may some day find yourselves hopeless. It's your choice. Everyone of you who are messing with Drugs can see how it's affecting your true care and love for anyone but yourselves. For your own sakes. Stop now before it's too late. Jesus Christ cares about you! He wants *you* to choose him. Don't forsake him. Draw close to him and *obey* him.

Dear Michael,

Don't rebel against your teachers and elders Michael. Work hard in school now. If your friends think you are a chicken if you don't misbehave don't worry about it. STAY AWAY FROM DRUGS AND ALL THOSE E.S.P. AND OTHER THINGS YOU ARE MESSING IN. REMEMBER THE THINGS I SPOKE TO YOU ABOUT WHEN I WALKED CLOSE TO GOD. REMEMBER HOW I CHANGED. God can change you too Michael. He can give you the peace you didn't have at home. Get close to him and *stay there!!* Discipline your mind while your still in school. Don't run wild like all the other kids.

GOD FORGIVE ME FOR NE-GLECTING YOU AND FOR BE-COMING SO COLD!! TAKE CARE OF MICHAEL AND MOM. HAVE MERCY ON MY SOUL. AMEN.

After finishing these two letters, Matt stuck the barrel of a .22 rifle in his mouth and pulled the trigger. *Don't make Matt's mistake.* There is help—and forgiveness—available to you and your friends.

How can you stop someone from committing suicide?

First, be aware of the following warning signs that the problem may be greater than normal ups and downs:

- Mood swings
- Signs of depression, such as: lack of concentration; deep-rooted boredom; withdrawal; eating too much or too little; lack of energy; self-criticism; negative thinking; feelings of guilt, shame, fear, or helplessness; rebellion; overconfidence; lack of fear of death
- Problems at school
- Problems communicating
- Any sudden change in behavior. A sudden improvement in attitude may mean he or she has made the decision to commit suicide and now feels a sense of relief or control
- Increased use of alcohol or drugs
- The giving away of personal property
- Self-destructive behavior
- Talk about suicide, particularly specifics of how it will be done

Second, know what to do if someone close to you talks about suicide:

- Always take talk about suicide seriously.
- Assure your friend of your concern and love. Also remind your friend that feelings of depression are natural and can be overcome with proper help. Try to convince him or her that suicide is a permanent solution for a temporary problem.
- Don't promise to keep secrets about suicidal talk or attempts if your friend won't seek help on his or her own.
- Offer to go with him or her to talk to a professional.

Third, know what to do if your friend makes specific plans to commit suicide:

- Tell the person you are not going to leave him or her alone and are calling for help, then do it!
- Call 9-1-1, the police, a suicide hot line, the mental health clinic, or your pastor or youth worker.
- Don't leave the person alone until professional help arrives. Don't try to handle the situation yourself. And don't put yourself in any unnecessary danger.

101

Professional Resources

If you have had long-lasting feelings of depression or thoughts of suicide on a regular basis, you need to talk to a professional.

Your first stop should be your family doctor. He or she can help you find out if there is a physical cause for your depression. Researchers have discovered that chemical imbalance in the brain often is the cause of clinical depression. Prescription drugs often easily correct the problem.

If you need emotional help, your pastor, youth director, or school counselor may be able to help you. If they can't, they will refer you to others who can. Always remember: there is hope!

And remember, too, that down times are normal, they're temporary, and they can be overcome with the right help. You don't ever have to be overcome. Believe it![1]

If, tragically, a friend of yours or someone you love does end his or her life, it's easy to feel that you somehow let that person down or that you could have done more to keep him or her from doing it. Judy and Charlie agonized over what they could have done to avert Terri's death. Such feelings of responsibility are normal—but seldom true.

Suicide is a personal choice made by the person who commits it. Only that person is ultimately responsible for his or her actions. And even then, many health-care professionals believe that suicide is an irrational act—sort of a "temporary insanity."

Can a Christian who commits suicide still go to heaven?

If this is truly the case, then the haunting question, Will a Christian who commits suicide still go to heaven? seems to be answered. We are judged on the basis of our ability to make rational decisions. And as we'll discuss later in chapter 21, we don't go to heaven because of our good deeds or go to hell because of our bad actions. Heaven and hell are determined by our decision to accept or reject Christ's offer of pardon.

It's a tough call, but we can be assured that God will treat each person with a careful balance of justice and mercy. (See chapter 4 for more on this.)

9

How Can a Person Deal with Dead Bodies?

You're here to do what?!" the receptionist at the Stone and Stone Chapel stammers.

"I'm here to watch an embalming. Mike made the arrangements."

"What do you want to do that for?" the woman questions as she stares at me through narrowed eyes. I can almost hear the sound of her suspicious brain cells: *Is this guy an inspector with the Indiana State Board of Health? . . . a serial killer? . . . somebody into kinky sex?*

"I'm writing a book about death."

"Oh. I never go back to the prep room." She shakes her head, shrugs her shoulders, and then goes back to reading the morning paper.

Mike Stone is not a stereotype of an "undertaker." He's twenty-eight and dressed like a young urban professional.

"Hi, Jim. I'm just beginning to prepare a body, so come right on back."

He leads me to a door that warns Danger: Health Risk. Employees Only Past This Point. Before opening it he explains, "We have two bodies in the preparation room today. One is a seventy-year-old woman who has already been prepared, dressed, and placed in her casket. The second one, which I'll be working on today, is an eighty-year-old woman who just died last night."

As he opens the door, my eyes first focus on a casket with the seventy-year-old. The colored floodlights above it give the typically pink glow that I'm familiar with. But then, out of the corner of my eye, I see a completely naked body lying on a stainless steel table. There is nothing pink or glowing about her yellowish-white skin and white hair.

"Here's a lab coat and an apron," Mike offers.

He puts on thick latex gloves—more like cleaning gloves than surgical gloves—and plastic goggles.

I feel uncomfortable looking at the body—I feel like I'm invading her privacy. So I maintain eye contact with Mike. "Are these precautions against AIDS?" I ask, indicating the gloves and goggles.

What's **embalming** **like?** "Well, actually we're more worried about hepatitis. It's a viral infection of the liver and is transmitted by blood. You can usually tell someone who's died of HIV. They'll be really thin. But you or I could have hepatitis right now and not know it, so we presume that every body is carrying some dangerous disease. Usually the hospital or health care facility will put an orange or green tag on their toe that says, 'Take Extra Precautions with Body Fluids.'

"The goggles are for the formaldehyde. You can go blind if you get it in your eyes."

Mike grabs a spray bottle—the kind glass cleaner comes in—and begins to spray the body from face to feet. "First we thoroughly disinfect the body and wipe out any fluids in the mouth, eyes, nose, genitals, and rectum with cotton. When a person dies all the muscles relax, so most people release the contents of their bladder at death."

The table has a one-inch lip around it, and water is constantly flowing from a hose at the head end to the drain at the feet end.

"The legal definition of embalming is disinfection,

preservation, and restoration. Restoration means making the body look more lifelike," Mike explains.

"After we've thoroughly washed the body, we begin setting features, or positioning the body as it will look in the casket."

He takes "eye caps," which look like large contact lenses, and smears them with "industrial-strength" petroleum jelly. He carefully pries open each eye, positions the plastic disc on the eyeball, and then closes each eye. "This keeps the eyes closed and keeps them moist so they don't dehydrate and disfigure.

"Next we want to raise vessels. If a person has lost a lot of weight, we want to puff up the body with embalming fluid." Mike takes a scalpel and makes a two-inch cut just above where the right leg connects to the body. I'm surprised at the lack of blood and lack of color of the muscles as Mike cuts through skin and muscle.

"Most of the blood has settled into the low spots at the back of the body," Mike explains. "I'm looking—actually feeling—for the femoral artery." He speaks with authority, and yet casually, as if he's teaching a biology class.

Do you mess your pants when you die?

"Arteries are pearl colored, but the veins running right beside them are gorged with blood. I'm going to tie a piece of surgery string around the artery." I'm amazed at how delicately his fingers work through the thick rubber gloves.

"Next, we'll make an incision just above the collar bone on the right side to find the jugular vein. We'll inject through the artery and drain through the vein." Again, there is no blood as he quickly locates the vein, which is dark blue, and ties surgical string around it.

"We'll use chemicals to dissolve the coagulated—or gelled—blood. The longer between death and embalming, the harder it is to embalm."

Mike turns to the "Duo-Tronic II" embalming pump. A large, five-gallon glass container sits on a metal housing with pressure gauge dials and switches for "Low/High" and "Pulsate," The sign above it warns: DANGER. Formaldehyde. Irritant and Potential Cancer Hazard. Personnel Only.

Mike adds about one gallon of water to the tank. "Next we'll add PH-A, which helps break up blood clots, and then DI-CEN, which is a co-injection. DI-CEN promotes formaldehyde penetration into the tissue. It also treats the water to make it the same pH factor as the body."

Do they really sew your eyes shut?

"I'm using HY-FORM, which is formaldehyde with the highest index or strength. The higher the index, the higher degree of fixative. The more fixative, the more rigid it makes the skin. The lower the index, the softer and more lifelike the flesh will feel. I'm using the highest index because she's eighty years old and probably has some clogged arteries. I want to get the most preserving action possible on the first try.

"Next I'll add some red coloring to give more natural flesh tones. Now, while that's mixing we'll open the artery."

He makes a small incision in the wall of the artery. "This is a cannula," he explains, reaching for a tool. It looks like a thick hypodermic needle with an air pump connector on the end. He inserts this into the artery, then ties it in place with more surgical thread. Mike then connects the hose from the pump to the cannula in the artery.

"The embalming machine can force fluid into the body up to thirty pounds per square inch. We'll set it on five pounds today. The machine can also pulsate to circulate the fluid just as the heart would have.

"Normally, I'd open the vein now, but I want to puff up the body since she's lost a lot of weight. The fluid expands the tissue, then sets up." Mike points to the veins on the woman's head. "See the veins on her temple rise," he says with almost reverence. The pulsating action of the machine makes the body seem alive for the first time. A lifelike pink glow begins to spread across her face and down her left side as we both watch with a sense of awe.

After a gallon of fluid has been pumped into the body, Mike opens the jugular vein to relieve the pressure. A red river of blood flows over her shoulder and cascades onto the table.

"Ah, do you have a bar stool I could sit on?" I try to ask casually, as I suddenly feel hot, out of breath, and weak in the knees. As Mike goes to get a chair, I suddenly realize this is not a science project. The *lub-dub, lub-dub* of the machine sounds like a heart, and the yellowish-white skin continues to look more alive. This is—or I should say *was*—somebody's sister, wife, mother, grandmother, or aunt.

When Mike returns, I eagerly sit down and try to control my emotions. "How did you feel when you prepared your first body?" (I'm hoping he felt this squeamish as well!)

"I've grown up in the business. As a little boy I watched my dad do this—it wasn't something gross, just something you have to do. I worked in here as much as I could in high school, so it was second nature. The funeral service is family oriented. There are a lot of second- and third-generation funeral homes. It's just like if your grandfather and your father ran a hardware store, you're more likely to carry on the family business.

"So it's no more different than shelving bolts and tools at the hardware. And sometimes it can be almost that impersonal. Here's a body without any clothes on. We're cutting into them—obviously with no anesthetic. You can lose the sense of personality. Not that we're disrespectful in any way, but it's just another body that needs to be embalmed.

"But it's really tough if it's a friend or associate in the community. Three of my friends from my high-school class had been drinking and were hit by a train and were killed. The mother of one of them called me and said, 'I want you to take care of my son.' That was really hard. There were times I was sweating, as white as a sheet, and had to leave and get some air.

"So, if you know them, it can be very emotional for the funeral director as well. My father and I worked on Grandma and Grandpa. People asked us, 'Wouldn't you want someone else to do it?'" (I was about to ask that question!)

Mike continued. "Our answer was no. I wouldn't want anyone else to do it. It's something that I can do that nobody else can do. You want to take care of your family, so it's kinda like a tribute to them.

"To be a sensitive funeral director, my dad says you must have a death in your own family once every six months. I've seen some funeral homes where you're just another number. So you have to watch out that you don't get caught up in just the mechanics. We have three funerals tomorrow, so we have to make sure schedules are worked out, vehicles ready, and so on. But when someone calls with a loved one who just died, that's more important to them than schedules—it's probably the most traumatic thing that's ever happened to them.

Why do people get stiff when they die?

"And there's an advantage in knowing the person. You know their features, their skin color, how they smile. People show emotions through their eyes, but when they're dead, it has to be through their mouth." Mike pushes up the corners of the woman's mouth. "So we try to work a bit of a smile into the face—to show a little emotion." He keeps working with the mouth. "The embalming fluid remains liquid, but the tissue begins to fixate, so you keep working to get just the right position of the body."

"When does rigor mortis set in?" I ask.

"From about eight hours to sixteen hours after the person dies. After death the cells continue to produce energy. When they begin to die they begin setting up. The stiffness peaks at about eight hours and then loosens up after another eight hours. So if you pick up a body and it's limp and loose, you can guess that the person has been dead for at least sixteen hours."

What does a dead body feel like?

I finally work up enough nerve to touch the body. The skin feels like an orange skin that has been left out at room temperature. After watching the body's blood drained out and poisonous chemicals pumped in, there's no question that there's no life left in this body.

Although Mike's schedule is full today, he takes extra time to make seven more incisions to try to embalm parts of her body that have been blocked off by blood clots. "Sometimes you can get a good embalming with just the groin incision and use only the femoral artery and vein. Unfortunately, we can't [do that] in the very elderly."

After Mike is fully convinced that the fluid has reached every part of the body, he begins tying off all the arteries and veins he has cut.

Finally Mike bathes the body from top to toe with disinfectant soap, washes down the table, and then shampoos her hair with Rave moisturizing shampoo, which promises to "restore moisture to dry hair." He combs out her hair and then applies Kalon Cosmetic Massage Cream to the face and hands. "It helps keep the moisture in."

"Tomorrow her beautician will come and fix her hair and make her up," Mike notes as he respectfully covers the body with a pink sheet, leaving the head uncovered.

"Is embalming mandatory?"

"Not in Indiana. But our policy here is 'no embalming, no public viewing.' Without embalming, a dead body can be deadly to those coming in contact with it. One woman committed suicide and wasn't found for three days—[she had been] in a very warm room—so she was in the advanced stages of decomposition. It was so bad that when you touched her skin, it fell off. So you certainly don't want to expose families to that kind of sight—or smell—without embalming.

Do you have

to be

embalmed?

"And then there are some bodies that are so badly injured or decomposed that you can't embalm them. You can only put them in a plastic body bag and seal it up."

Mike turns to clean his instruments in the sink and then lays them in a tray of disinfectant. He carefully washes his gloves before removing them.

"Working here, you're reminded of your own mortality every day. Maybe I see that more than other people my age. Most of my friends are thinking about careers and advancement—the last thing they think about is death. But I deal with it every day.

"How can people work in this business and not be Christians?" he asks, staring at the body on the table. "And how can people stand at a casket with no hope of eternal life? You ask a lot of questions in this business." (We'll talk about some of those questions in the next chapter.)

PART FOUR

*How are you supposed
to react to death?*

I don't understand the problem," Mr. Norman said defensively as Mr. Coldwater waved Friday's issue of the Lakeshore Sentinel.

"The front page has two obituaries. OK, I see the need for that, but what about this editorial: 'Don't Bury Our Feelings.' Are you saying that I don't allow students to express their feelings? I gave half the senior class time off to go to Brian's funeral, and we'll do the same Monday for Renee's."

"But we need more help in dealing with these deaths," Lori defended her editorial. "Central brought in counselors to help kids work through the grief process."

"That's where I disagree, young lady!" the principal countered. "It's much healthier to keep this school on as normal a schedule as possible than to have some kind of giant group therapy session!"

"Well, maybe that's what we need!" Lori nearly shouted.

Mr. Norman tried to intervene. "With all due respect, Mr. Coldwater, we don't make news, but we do try to report it accurately. The facts are two students are dead, and an entire school is trying to sort out their feelings about those deaths. I think it's our job to help students recover from it."

"Let me remind you of your job, Mr. Norman. And that is to make sure that the Sentinel—" But Mr. Coldwater was cut off in midsentence by the whine of police sirens. All attention shifted out the windows as three police cars and an ambulance swarmed onto the vacant lot between the school and the new housing development.

"What's going on?" Kevin wanted to know as he grabbed the department's 35-mm camera and headed for the door.

"Take it easy, Jimmy Olson!" Mr. Norman cautioned as they all watched the officers and paramedics fan out over the lot. One seemed to find something in the tall weeds and then all converged on the spot. The paramedics ran back to the ambulance and returned with a stretcher.

"Well, they don't have their guns drawn, so it's probably safe to check it out, Kevin. Just don't get your nose for news in the way of whatever it is."

Kevin ran out the front door, his heart pounding with excitement and his head throbbing with possibilities: A drug stash . . . loot from a bank holdup . . . a UFO landing spot . . . No, those wouldn't explain the ambulance.

"Hey, you! Stay back!" one of the officers shouted. Kevin stopped and quickly focused the telephoto lens on what seemed to be the center of attention. He could barely make out what it was through the viewfinder as he started shooting. One of the officers had gone back to his car and come back with a large roll of yellow plastic tape with CRIME SCENE—STAY OUT printed along its length.

"What's happening?" Kevin shouted to him.

"Just don't come any nearer." The police were busily shooting pictures, and the paramedics casually walked back to the ambulance empty-handed.

Kevin spotted a mother and a small boy standing outside their house on the edge of the field. If I can't get anything official, I can at least talk to some possible eyewitnesses, *he thought. Kevin made a large circle around the crime scene and ran toward the house.*

"Excuse me," he gasped, trying to catch his breath. "I'm Kevin Farra from the high-school paper. Do you know what's going on?"

"My son," she began as she tightly held the preschooler, "was playing in the vacant lot when he said he found a girl sleeping in the field."

"She didn't have any clothes on," the boy added.

"Well, I went out to see, and that's when I found . . ." The woman's voice trailed off. "It was just awful. Why would anyone want to do that to anyone? Just awful. They had cut her throat and cut a big cross in her chest."

Suddenly two police officers interrupted. "Mrs. Norris?" The woman nodded. "I'm Sergeant Ryan, and this is my partner, Patrolman Smythe. We need to talk with you for a few minutes about what you and your son saw this afternoon. Privately." Kevin started to walk away when the sergeant called out to him. "Suppose you tell me what you're doing out here with a camera."

"I'm the editor of the school paper."

Ryan wrote down Kevin's name and phone number in a notebook. "You didn't see anything—remember that, Farra."

The mother, son, and two officers went into the house,

leaving Kevin feeling guilty for no reason at all. By that time the news staff and half the sixth-hour study hall had gathered around the "crime scene" perimeter.

"What's happening, Kevin?" Mr. Norman asked as he huddled with the four editors. "Keep it down, I don't want the news out yet."

Kevin barely whispered what he had uncovered.

"Now listen," Mr. Norman warned. "How we handle this can either help or hinder the killer's capture, so I don't want you to say anything about it to anyone. Have you got that? We'll talk about it Monday."

"Was she nude?" Kathy asked, paying no attention to Mr. Norman.

Kevin looked at Mr. Norman. "Why do you want to know?" the teacher asked Kathy.

"Because if she was, I know who did it!"

10
What Do You Say at a Funeral?

At the funeral of Brian McCarthy, Kevin and Lori stood in silence—not sure what to say to each other or to the two hundred other silent teens around them. What do you say at a funeral? seems to be a common question. And the simplest answer is:

That's right! Often the best thing to say is nothing—a shared tear, a squeezed hand, a hug, or just being there during this time of grief is often the most helpful thing.

Jim Stone, who has been a funeral director for more than thirty years, admits he still doesn't have pat answers for the plea, "I'm hurting and I don't know what to do."

"I usually tell people in the mourning process, 'Say what your heart tells you to say.' That's pretty safe. Most of all, don't have a prepared speech. Be sensitive enough to go with the flow, and say whatever you feel is needed at the time.

"Many times teens are looking for clues for what to say or do, so each funeral has a different emotional response.

What shouldn't you say at a funeral?

"For instance, hysteria feeds hysteria, and so we may have a very emotional service. Not that the teens are disrespectful in any way, but there is a lot of outward expression—crying and touching the deceased. I've even seen people kiss the body on the forehead or mouth. You won't catch me doing that, but I don't discourage it. At other times there are just as strong emotions, but it's very quiet and subdued.

"Although teens don't always know how to act or how to express themselves at a funeral, I've never seen any joking or laughing or a party attitude. They've always been very respectful because death is a very sobering thing.

"But, again, if you follow what your heart is telling you, you're usually safe."

There are some things that you shouldn't say:

Never Say "Passed Away"

No one seems to *die* in our culture. They've simply been "called home," "given up the ghost," "returned to dust," "gone the way of all mortal flesh," flown "to their heavenly reward," "crossed over the Jordan," "travelled on to Glory," or "moved upstairs" to "sing in the heavenly choir."

The less religious are said to be "on ice," "six feet under," "pushing up daisies," and "shoveling coal." "Their meter has expired." They've "breathed their last," "met the Grim Reaper," "keeled over," "bit the big one," "kicked the bucket," "bought the farm," "cashed in their chips," "closed up shop," "made the final deadline," "gone home feet first," "shuffled off to Buffalo," and "brought down the final curtain." "The fat lady has sung," and "Elvis has left the theater."

Actually, they're D-E-A-D!

Jim Stone continues, "One of the most important reasons for a funeral is to help the family and friends realize that their loved one has died. Christians do have the hope that the one they love has gone to his eternal reward, but as a funeral director I must help them cope with the fact that the earthly relationship is over.

"Friends and family can help overcome this natural denial mechanism by using the words *died* or *death*. This isn't always easy, but it is very necessary in the process of completing the earthly relationship. We're not being honest—psychologically or spiritually—to try to lessen what has occurred by avoiding 'the D-word.'"

As we'll learn in the next chapter, the first step in dealing with grief is to admit that there is something to grieve about.

Never Say, "I understand; I know how you feel."

Even if we've experienced an identical loss—such as we've both lost a grandparent—there are many things that we don't "understand" or "know": What kind of relationship did our friend have with his or her grandparent? Maybe the two were very close or maybe they only saw each other on Christmas. What were the last words spoken? Were they loving or harsh? What kinds of questions, thoughts, and feelings are churning in our friend's mind? What is our friend's concept of life after death?

We really can't know exactly what another person is feeling! But we can be a source of real healing in the mourning process by saying how we felt: "When my grandmother died I felt like . . ." In this way, we're letting our friend know that we've experienced a similar loss and are allowing *him* or *her* the freedom to tell us how *he* or *she* feels.

Never Say, "Don't cry; be strong."

Our friend is already struggling with overwhelming feelings. (We'll talk about them in the next chapter.) We musn't make the person feel that he or she is weak, immature, or not handling the death well by adding shame and guilt to the emotional load. We need to allow our friend to express feelings.

Is it OK to cry out loud at a funeral?

Jim Stone comments, "I've noticed that guys today are much more open to express their emotions. I see that as a healthy sign."

On the other hand, we need to be careful not to make our friend feel guilty for *not* showing outward emotion. He or she may still be in the shock or denial stage that we'll talk about in the next chapter.

Never Say, "You don't have to talk about the details of the death."

We often think that by asking a survivor about the details of the death, we'll cause more pain and sorrow. So we carefully avoid words like *cancer, suicide, drowning, shooting,* or *AIDS*.

Surprisingly, most survivors want to talk about how their loved one died. My wife's mother must have told the story of how her husband died at least ten times while the family was gathered at her home during the days before the funeral. But each time she told the story—how he said she better call the ambulance, how he collapsed on the dining room floor and cut his forehead on the telephone stand, how she tried to initiate CPR that she had seen on TV— she seemed to gain emotional strength and comfort.

Should you talk about how someone died?

Talking about the details also helps move our friend past the denial stage and into the mourning process.

Never Quote Scripture or Sentimental Phrases

If you've read any of my previous books, you know that I have the utmost respect for God's Word. But mourners aren't ready for pat answers and trite clichés.

For instance, while delivering our daughter, my wife, Lois, vomited from the anesthetic and breathed the fluid into her lungs. It's called aspiradic pneumonia, and the last three women at St. Mary's Hospital with the condition had died within hours.

And so I sat in the intensive care unit for five days, not sure if little Faith would have a mother and I would still have a wife. People who came to visit me were very kind, but they would only stop by long enough to quote a Bible verse and then leave me to sit alone for several more agonizing hours.

My undergraduate work was in theology, so I knew all the verses—and I resented the hit-and-run sermons. I wasn't ready for "answers" at that point. I needed someone to sit with me in that lonely waiting room. Fortunately,

Peggy Ott came by with a deck of Uno cards and spent one afternoon playing cards with me. She cared enough to just spend time with me. That was more helpful than all the Bible verses.

Again, don't misunderstand me. There is a time for God's Word. But often people in the initial stages of grief need our ears more than our mouth. And sometimes they just need our warm body in the same room—and nothing more.

Most important, simply express your love for them. And then wait for them to tell you what they want to talk about.

11

When Does It Stop Hurting?

A fifteen year old wrote on the survey:

> I feel sad. My grandmother died three years ago. I live right next to her house. Now my aunt lives in it. I spent my childhood at her house with my cousins. Every time I go in, I want to cry. I'm not sure what to do. I got her dog, Taffy, when she died. After she died, Taffy would go down to the house and wait on the porch for Grandma to let her in.
>
> I'm not sure if there is life after death. All I know is that I miss my grandmother. I never even got to say good-bye. She had died in the afternoon. When I came home from school, I went to her house. She wasn't there. My uncle told me that she was in the hospital, but he didn't tell me that she had died. My mom and my sister and I didn't find out until about eight o'clock that night that she had died.
>
> **How can I tell her good-bye and that I love and miss her?**

Can you feel this young person's pain of loss? That's what grief is—an emotion of loss. Perhaps you have felt it when a parent moved away after a divorce, when you broke up with a boyfriend or girlfriend, or when you moved away from your old neighborhood. Even losing a valued object (such as a class ring or some other memento) or an important ball game creates a sense of grief. There's a feeling of separation and loss.

Grief and love are two very similar emotions—if you are capable of love, you are capable of grief. Only a person who never loves never grieves. When you love someone, you feel a oneness and fulfillment with that person. But you also open yourself up to the possibility for grief—when he or she breaks up with you, moves away, or dies. The relationship is over, and that strong emotion of love transforms into equally strong grief.

Why do you hurt when someone you love dies?

Grief, then, is the flip side of love. Love expresses emotional oneness; grief expresses emotional separation.

Mourning is the long, painful process of working through that grief. (In other words, grief is what we feel; mourning is how we respond to it.)

Throughout *Sex Is Not a Four-Letter Word,* I keep reminding my readers that the emotional roller-coaster ride of adolescence is normal. It's natural to feel up one day and down the next. It's OK to be ahead or behind young people our age in physical development. And a million other teens are experiencing the same feelings.

But adolescent emotions do feel "abnormal" and "unnatural" when we're experiencing them for the first time. In the same way, the strong feelings of grief may seem frightening when we first feel the full force of this powerful emotion. But like other emotions, it's normal, natural, and OK. And like adolescent development, grief follows a general pattern.

Stage One: Shock, Numbness, Disbelief (one to three days)[1]

Remember Lori's reaction when she heard of Brian's death? "I just can't believe it!" When we're first told that someone we love has died, there is an immediate sense of shock and disbelief. Like denial in the dying process, disbelief insulates our emotions so we can deal with immediate demands: notifying friends and relatives, calling our pastor, letting the school know we'll be out for a few days, cleaning the house for visitors, and so on.

Once the initial numbness wears off, it's normal to cry—everything from watery eyes to uncontrollable sobbing. Crying is a healthy emotional expression of grief, so don't feel that you're being weak. And ignore ignorant clichés, like "smile and the whole world smiles with you, cry and you cry alone."

Why don't you feel anything right after someone you love dies?

And it's not unusual to feel anger toward the person for dying: "How dare you leave me to suffer like this!" You may feel angry at the medical staff for not saving your loved one's life—even though you know the doctors and nurses did everything possible. And as I mentioned in chapter 6, it's not uncommon to feel angry at God—even if you're a very devout believer. It's OK!

It's not unusual, then, to feel these emotions, but it *is* unhealthy to deny them. For instance, Andrew's first child was born dead. When I visited him the next day, the burly factory worker proudly announced that he hadn't shed a tear. "My little girl's bouncing on Jesus' knee in heaven, so why should I be sad?"

But as months and years went by, Andrew's unresolved grief and anger began to come out as verbal and physical abuse against his wife (he tried to run her down with his truck), coworkers, and even his second child. Andrew had tried to plug up the mouth of a volcano of emotions, but the pressure simply blew a gaping hole out the side of the mountain.

I should point out that being a Christian doesn't exempt a person from grief and mourning. Jesus said, "Blessed are those who mourn, for they will be comforted" (Matthew 5:4, NIV). "Jesus wept" at the tomb of his friend Lazarus, even though he was planning to raise him from the dead (John 11:35). Jesus also went away by himself to mourn the execution of John the Baptist even though he knew his cousin was now in heaven (Matthew 14:13).

Why do some people, when they've lost someone close to them, act like nothing happened?

The apostle Paul doesn't glorify death either. He calls it an enemy, even though he assures his readers that if they believe in Christ, they will live forever (1 Corinthians 15:12-58).

The hope that we will see loved ones in heaven doesn't eliminate the intense pain of losing that earthly relationship!

So, in review, all these things are normal:

- Shock
- Disbelief, denial
- Numbness
- Weeping, sobbing
- Anger

Allow these emotions to be expressed to those you can trust with your feelings—your best friend, family, youth worker, or pastor.

Stage Two: Painful Longing and Preoccupation with Memories and Mental Images (up to one year)

We often think that the funeral is the hardest time for the survivors, so we may bring in food, visit the family, and attend the funeral. But afterward, we assume they've started the work of putting their lives back together.

Actually, stage two becomes most intense between the second and fourth week after the funeral. The following experiences are strong for about the first three months and then gradually begin to diminish over the next six months to a year:

- A painful longing to be with and talk with the dead person
- A preoccupation with the death (you can't think of anything else)
- Memories of the dead person
- Mental images of the dead person
- Sensing that the dead person is in the same room
- Sadness
- Tearfulness
- Inability to sleep
- Lack of concentration
- Loss of appetite
- Loss of interest in things you once enjoyed
- Irritability
- Restlessness

Again, these are normal reactions and nothing to be ashamed of. We may also have a difficult time maintaining the grades we're used to getting. Don't view this as being a failure or mentally undisciplined. Death puts a tremendous strain on not only our emotions but our mind as well.

The sense of grief is even greater if the death was untimely (a teen or a young adult), if it occurred through a tragic or violent means (accident, suicide, or murder), or if it was of someone the survivor was very dependent upon, such as a parent or best friend.

For instance, fifteen-year-old Jason was driving a golf cart with his little brother, Justin, sitting in the back. Jason was driving faster than he should around the yard. He made a sharp turn, causing his brother to fly from the cart and smash his head into a cement step. Justin died instantly. Jason, who apparently felt completely responsible, didn't speak to anyone for three weeks following the accident. In a case like this, professional help may be necessary. (Resources and a listing of unhealthy grief symptoms are listed in Appendix B.)

Funeral director Jim Stone suggests some ways to deal with that painful longing to say good-bye to the one you loved. "I always ask the living, 'Did you get everything said that you wanted to say? If not, here are a couple suggestions: Write the deceased a letter telling them what you wanted to say but never said, seal it in an envelope, and put it in the casket. Or if appropriate, you may want to read it at the funeral.'

After my grandfather died, I would walk into a room and almost believe he was there. Is that normal?

"I also suggest people leave a little memento—something that meant a lot between the two—in the casket. And if they don't want it seen by others, we'll put it out of sight by the deceased's feet."

Grief seems to come in waves. One day we'll feel that we're finally over our loved one's death. But then smelling his favorite cologne, hearing his favorite song on the radio, or coming to a birthday or holiday will trigger overwhelming grief once more. These tidal waves are especially intense and painful at night when we're not distracted by school, after-school jobs, sports, watching TV, or hanging out with our friends.

And the mourning process may not progress neatly from one stage to the next, as a Christian author, C. S. Lewis, explains regarding the death of his wife:

> Tonight all the hells of young grief have opened again, the mad words, the bitter resentment, the fluttering in the stomach, the nightmare unreality, the wallowing in tears. For in grief, nothing "stays put." One keeps on emerging from a phase, but it always recurs. Round and round. Everything repeats. Am I going in circles, or dare I hope I am on a spiral? But if a spiral, am I going up or down it?[2]

Do you ever stop hurting after someone you love dies?

Accepting the fact that grief is a long—up to one year—process may be difficult. As we discussed in chapter 8, we live in an "instant" society: instant drinks, microwave popcorn, and fast food. We're tempted to think that our emotional state should change in thirty seconds or less.

And don't be afraid to turn to professionals for help during this difficult time. Your doctor may prescribe sleeping pills or tranquilizers so you can sleep nights. School counselors, youth workers, or pastors can provide emotional support and suggestions for overcoming this time of loss. If they can't, they can refer you to those who can.

Stage Three: Resolution and Resumption of Ordinary Life Activities (within one year of death)

Starting at about six months, most of us will begin getting back into our normal activities. We'll continue to be broadsided by occasional waves of grief as described in stage two. But these will become less and less frequent, even though they may be just as intense.

Stage three involves:

130

- Acceptance of the death
- Decreasing sadness
- The ability to recall past experiences with the deceased with pleasure rather than pain
- Resuming ordinary activities.

In summary, grief is a normal—but sometimes confusing and uncontrollable—emotion. And mourning (dealing with grief) is a long, painful process.

But remember: you *will* once again enjoy living and loving; you *will* get your appetite back; the pain *will* diminish; you *will* be able to sleep soundly again; and you *will* be able to enjoy pleasant memories of the deceased. It *will*, however, take time.

12
Can You Ever Really Be Prepared for Death?

Two tombstones stand side by side in the Pleasantville Cemetery in Houghton, New York: one at attention, guarding the remains of twenty-four-year-old Samuel Glenn Root, a U. S. Marine Corps corporal; the other as a silent witness to the violent death of Jean Root Aldrich, thirty-one.

Sam had three years to prepare for his death from AIDS. His sister Jean probably never felt the fatal blow to her neck.

Sam's medical file is a thick catalog of rare diseases: aspergillus pneumonia, cerebral toxoplasmosis, chronic sinusitis, cytomegalo viral retinitis, hepatitis, herpes simplex virus, oral thrush, and pneumocystis caninili. For the last year and a half, Sam was completely blind due to AIDS-related diseases.

His sister Jean didn't have the "luxury" of three years' notice. She had come out of her house to scold some neighborhood children for throwing rocks. Silently, a man who had been drinking all day crept up behind her, locked his fists together, and struck her on the neck, rupturing a primary artery to the brain. The autopsy revealed that she died almost instantly from severe internal bleeding.

Out of these tragedies come lessons for all of us.

Value Life, Value Each Other

One of Sam's greatest concerns, after being diagnosed as HIV-positive, was for good relationships between his parents, his four brothers and six sisters, and his nieces and nephews. The normally soft-spoken young man became aggressive in making sure that relationships were right. "Hey, you guys, value life and each other."

He frequently asked his mother, "How are you and Dad getting along?" He tried hard to get to know his father, who during his childhood years had been a long-distance trucker weekdays and a pastor on the weekends.

Because none of us knows our date of death, we need to work at keeping our relationships with our parents, brothers and sisters, and friends in good shape.

Will the last thing we remember saying to a deceased person be loving and kind or hateful and hurtful? What will be the condition of our relationships at death?

We need to remember the words of Scripture:

> Stop lying to each other; tell the truth, for we are parts of each other and when we lie to each other we are hurting ourselves. If you are angry, don't sin by nursing your grudge. Don't let the sun go down with you still angry—get over it quickly. . . .
>
> Stop being mean, bad-tempered and angry. Quarreling, harsh words, and dislike of others should have no place in your lives. Instead be kind to each other, tenderhearted, forgiving one another, just as God has forgiven you because you belong to Christ. (Ephesians 4:25-26, 31-32)

Make a Difference

While in the HIV Unit of Balboa Navy Hospital, Sam was an eager guinea pig for experimental treatments. He felt that if he could contribute to AIDS research, somehow his life would have counted for something.

Rabbi Harold Kushner points out that:

133

Our souls are not hungry for fame, comfort, wealth, or power. Those rewards create almost as many problems as they solve. Our souls are hungry for meaning, for the sense that we have figured out how to live so that our lives matter, so that the world will be at least a little bit different for our having passed through it. . . .

How will the world be different after I'm gone?

If a person lives and dies and no one notices, if the world continues as it was, was that person ever really alive?

I am convinced that it is not the fear of death, of our lives ending, that haunts our sleep so much as the fear that as far as the world is concerned, we might as well never have lived.[1]

Here are fifty ways to let the world know that you lived:

1. Make people laugh.
2. Be a friend to people who don't have many friends.
3. Smile at everyone you meet.
4. Be generous with encouragement.
5. Build up peoples' self-esteem with sincere compliments.
6. Listen intently when people are talking; look them in the eyes.
7. Treat everyone you meet with love and respect (beginning with your mom and dad, brother and sister).
8. Forgive and forget.
9. Be polite and say thank you to waitresses and store clerks.

10. Read to those who can't read.
11. Better yet, teach people how to read.
12. Volunteer at a church.
13. Volunteer at a community organization.
14. Volunteer at a hospital.
15. Volunteer at a nursing home.
16. Volunteer at a school.
17. Teach a day care or church school class.
18. Become a tutor.
19. Sponsor a child through an international relief organization.
20. Learn to save a life with CPR.
21. Give blood.
22. Sign a donor's card (see the section of this chapter titled "Give Life at Your Death").
23. Do things for others that they can't do, such as grocery shopping.
24. Or mowing their lawns.
25. Or walking their dogs.
26. Or housecleaning.
27. Or tuning up their cars, changing the oil, etc.
28. Or raking leaves.
29. Or putting in/taking out storm windows.
30. Or shoveling snow.
31. Be a pen pal to an overseas military or missionary child or teen.
32. Visit people in the hospital.
33. Visit people in nursing homes.
34. Write a poem or short story.
35. Write a letter to the editor.
36. Write a letter to your legislators.
37. If you're eighteen or older, register and vote.
38. Work for a political candidate.
39. Spread your faith.
40. Don't spread gossip.
41. Or STDs.

42. Share this book with a friend.
43. Listen to a friend who is depressed.
44. Plant trees and flowers.
45. Become your family's official photographer and biographer.
46. Recycle.
47. Bake cookies for shut-ins.
48. Don't let friends drive drunk.
49. Help friends kick some habits (see chapter 5).
50. Send thank-you notes to people who have made your world a little bit better for their having passed through it.

135

Joyce Landorf sums it up well: "The big question is not 'Will I die?' but, 'How shall I live until I die?'"[2]

Plan Ahead

There are many ways that we can plan for our death—and doing that can give us a bit of a feeling of control over something we have little control over.

Sam began making plans for the rest of his life and beyond. He named Jean's children as his beneficiaries—the ones who would get the money from his life insurance at death.

Sam didn't have a "last will and testament," but a will is especially important for parents. It allows Mom and Dad to select the family that will care for you in the event that they both die.

To the teen who asked, **"My mom's a single parent. If she dies, will I have to live in an orphanage?"** the answer depends on whether your parent has a will. When there is no will, the court system in most states will determine

If you die and haven't made out a will, who will get your belongings?

where the children will be placed and who gets any money and property.

If you have some valuable or sentimental things that you would like to leave to certain family or friends, then it would be best to have a will. But that's not always necessary for teens. If you write out your desires and have two witnesses sign the paper, that should hold up as directions for who gets your CD player, your tape collection, or your guitar. Anything more complicated such as cash, property, children, etc., needs a professionally prepared will.

What's a living will?

Sam also made it known that in the event of cardiac arrest he did not want to be resuscitated. This is often known as a "living will." The following is a model drawn up by Concern for the Dying:

> Death is as much a reality as birth, growth, maturity, and old age. It is the one certainty of life. If the time comes when I, [name], can no longer take part in decisions for my own future, let this statement stand as an expression of my wishes, while I am still of sound mind. If the situation should arise in which there is no reasonable expectation of my recovery from physical or mental disability, I request that I be allowed to die and not be kept alive by artificial means or heroic measures. I do, however, ask that medication be mercifully administered to me to alleviate suffering even though this may shorten my remaining life. This statement is made after careful consideration and is in accordance with my strong convictions and beliefs. I want the wishes and directions here expressed carried out to the extent permitted by law. Insofar as they are not legally enforceable, I hope that those to whom this Will is addressed will regard themselves as morally bound by these provisions.[3]

Living wills are still controversial and not accepted in all states. Before signing, one should carefully discuss the implications with his immediate family, pastor, and doctor.

Sam also made it known that he wanted his body to be cremated (burned to ashes) and his funeral to be a "home-going celebration."

Jim Stone, the funeral director we met in chapter 10, observes that "the trend is away from what we would call 'traditional' funeral services. Thirty years ago there was always one or two days of visitation and then a huge, long funeral. Today, especially on the two coasts, the trend is toward direct cremation with no calling hours and no funeral."

Can I decide what happens to my body after I die?

Time and money may be the reasons for the trend. A traditional funeral with embalming, casket, visitation hours, services, limos, burial vaults, and cemetery lots can cost several thousand dollars, while cremation is a fraction of the cost. To ship Sam's body from California to New York would have cost thousands of dollars beyond that.

But Mike Stone believes that cremation may be more "costly" in the long run. "There's a real advantage to an open casket and a funeral service. Without being able to see and touch the dead body your mind will play tricks on you. There's no confirmation that your loved one is really dead."

"That's why I object to the way cremation is handled in the Western world," Jim adds. "The body is simply shipped to the crematorium, and like Mike mentioned, there's no reality of the death. In India, however, the cremation takes place in a public place, and the family often lights the funeral pyre. In South Africa, the funeral is often held at the crematorium. So in the Eastern world, the psychological need to see the body 'laid to rest' is satisfied."

Sam's parents initially objected to the idea of cremation, but then chose to follow their son's desire. We can make our wishes known about how we want our body disposed of, such as in-ground or above-ground burial or cremation. (When my friend Bob Harris discovered he had terminal cancer, he went so far as to have an Amish cabinetmaker build a beautiful, solid wood casket to his precise specifications. Bob kept the coffin in his back room and joked, "If I whip this cancer, I can always use it as a guest room." Unfortunately, he did die a few months later.)

Can I donate my body when I die?

So if you have strong preferences, do discuss them with your family, since in most states final decisions are in the hands of your immediate family.

Give Life at Your Death

Because Sam's body was infected with AIDS, and Jean's body was used as evidence in a murder trial, donations of vital organs and tissue were impossible. But those are exceptional cases.

An estimated twenty thousand Americans need transplanted organs and tissue each year. Eighteen thousand are waiting for kidneys, fifteen hundred for livers, more than two thousand for hearts. But less than one-tenth of those numbers will have organs donated at another's death.

The Uniform Anatomical Gift Act, which is recognized in all fifty states, allows a person to donate (1) all organs/tissues, (2) specific organs/tissues, or (3) the entire body for medical research. Donors of all ages are needed for bone, eyes, hearts, heart valves, kidneys, livers, lungs, pancreases, and skin.

To become a donor at your death, you need to sign an organ donor card and have it witnessed by two people (your parents, if you're under eighteen, or someone in your immediate family). The most important step is to discuss your wishes with your immediate family since they will have to be the ones to give consent for your organs and tissue to be donated.

All the costs of transplanting your organs and tissues will be paid by the receiver's health insurance—it won't cost your family anything for you to be a donor. And organ and tissue donation will not disfigure your body if your parents or immediate family want to have your body viewed at the funeral.

139

The following is an excerpt from a letter sent by the Indiana Organ Procurement Organization, Inc., to the family of a young girl who died tragically.

We were able to use your daughter's heart, kidneys, liver, and corneas for transplantation. I would like to give you some information on the recipients of your generosity.

Your daughter's heart was transplanted into a fifty-nine-year-old Indiana woman who had been extremely ill in the hospital prior to her surgery. She is doing well and looks forward to returning home to enjoy her retirement and her grandchildren.

Her liver was transplanted into a fifty-year-old Indiana woman. Unfortunately, she did not survive the surgery. I'm sure that her husband and three grown children are grateful that she was at least given the chance for a better life. This is all she wanted.

Her right kidney was transplanted into a thirty-two-year-old woman from Boston. She is doing very well and looking forward to the future with her fiancé.

Her left kidney was transplanted into a fifty-year-old man from California. He will soon be able to return to his career as a county administrator. He also enjoys traveling and movies.

Although I do not have any follow-up information on the corneas, they can be used to restore the sight of two people.

Hopefully this information will help lessen the pain that you have and can be a memory of your daughter that you will cherish. Thank you again for offering us a very special opportunity to help many others to live longer with a much better quality of life. It is this thoughtfulness for others at a very difficult time which allows transplantation to occur.[4]

Make Things Right with Your Maker

Sam and Jean had been raised in a Christian home, but as young people they both had turned their back on God.

Sam was always sensitive, artistic, and a lover of music. Because he was more interested in reading than sports, teachers and classmates alike labeled him "different." Sam joined the Marine Corps to prove his manhood, but he eventually turned to the homosexual community for understanding and compassion.

After running away from home, Jean lived as a prostitute while living with a drug dealer. She suffered the consequences of this dangerous life-style by being gang raped, threatened at knife point, and brutally beaten. She had four children with four different partners.

It was a long road from a small country church parsonage in Wisconsin for both Sam and Jean.

After being diagnosed with HIV, Sam began his trip back to God. "I don't know why God wants me because I don't have much left to offer him," Sam questioned. But he admitted that he was "loved back to the Lord" through the unconditional love of his parents. "My mom told me,

'You can hurt me—and you have—but you can never do anything that will keep me from loving you.'"

In the same way his wayward sister was loved back to God. The Sunday before her murder, she had attended church with her family, seemed genuinely joyful about her restored faith, and sang in a trio Sunday night with her mother and another woman. Monday she brought her children to Vacation Bible School and stayed to help. By nine-thirty that night she was in the hospital morgue.

The uncertainty of life is the reason the Bible claims, "Right now God is ready to welcome you. Today he is ready to save you" (2 Corinthians 6:2). (We'll talk more about knowing God in chapter 21.)

The idea of planning for your death may seem a little strange—it certainly did when I was a teen. It may even seem frightening. One teen wrote, **"Death is really scary because you never know when you will die."**

How can you make the idea of death not so scary?

But making plans does eliminate some of the questions asked: What will happen to my body after I'm dead? Will they take my eyes out even if I don't want it done? Who gets my tapes and stuff when I die?

Now that I'm married and have a son who just reached the big "one-oh" and a daughter who's in her teens, I guess I think more about death—especially before leaving on a trip. So in the top drawer of our fireproof file cabinet is an "In Case of Death" file. It's reassuring to know that if Lois and I come face-to-face with a Mack truck:

- We have a will that will make sure our children are well cared for by a loving couple in our church.
- Our organs will be donated (if they survive the crash).

- We'll have our favorite songs sung and Scripture read at our funeral since we've left a list.
- What money we leave behind will go toward college scholarships to students at Indiana Wesleyan University.

I'm not planning to make national news this week ("Author and Wife Die in Fiery Car Crash"), but if I do, I'm as prepared as I can humanly be. And that takes a lot of the fear away.

But the most reassuring thoughts are found on Jean's and Sam's tombstones.

On Jean's, a woman suddenly murdered: "My times are in your [God's] hands."

And on Sam's, a young man who died in slow motion: "Death has been swallowed up in victory."

PART FIVE

Is there really life after death?

The Saturday and Sunday editions of the city paper rationed out small bits and pieces of information about the murder: fifteen-year-old girl . . . found dead near Lakeshore Estates . . . identity being withheld pending notification of relatives . . . no further details . . . believed to be a Lakeshore sophomore. Finally, early Sunday evening the local TV station dangled one last detail before its viewers: "Police identify dead Lakeshore High School student. Details at eleven."

Kevin had spent Saturday and Sunday almost immobilized from not knowing who the girl was. He and Nate had stayed after school Friday trying to enlarge the photos he had shot at the scene of the crime. All the photos either were out of focus or had someone blocking a clear view of the victim's face.

Other questions messed with Kevin's mind: How should the *Sentinel* report the third death in less than two weeks? . . . How will Coldwater handle the death . . . and the coverage of the death? . . . Why do the police and Mr. Norman want us to keep everything so hush-hush? . . . How is Lori taking this?

Kevin was even more confused about Lori's behavior and what it meant than he was about "who done it" to whom. Several times during the weekend he considered calling her, but he always found an excuse not to. But still, he was concerned about his "friend." Yeah, *he thought,* that's all she is—a friend.

Kevin's heart pounded each time the Sunday night movie was interrupted with the teaser of "film at eleven." What a manipulative way to get the station's ratings up, *he thought as the clock on the VCR glowed "11:00."*

The jarring ring of the phone broke Kevin's intense concentration on the opening graphics and music.

"Hi, Kevin? This is Lori. My folks went to bed early, and I just couldn't take hearing who was murdered alone. So do you mind if I watch the news with you—at least over the phone?"

"Yeah, that's OK," Kevin said. "I thought about calling you this weekend—oh, here's the news."

"The body of fifteen-year-old Traci Yamagishi, daughter of George and Donna Yamagishi, was found Friday by a neighborhood child in a vacant lot adjacent to Lakeshore Estates.

"Police are offering few details except to say that foul play is suspected in the death of the Lakeshore High School sophomore.

"Anyone with any information about the death of Traci Yamagishi is asked to call CrimeStoppers at 1-800-555-STOP."

Kevin cut the announcer short with the TV remote. "Did you know her?" he asked.

"I don't think so," Lori replied. There was a long silence over the phone line. "Still, it really scares me to know that someone was killed next door to the school."

"*Yeah,*" *Kevin empathized.* "*How have you been this weekend?*"

"*Oh, I've used a lot of Kleenex.*"

"*Me too.*" *Kevin was surprised that he had admitted shedding any tears to Lori, but somehow he didn't feel that uncomfortable about it.*

"*Really?*" *Lori asked with a smile in her voice that seemed to say she was glad to hear it.*

"*Yeah, but you don't have to write that up for the paper. I do have my hard-boiled-editor image to uphold, you know.*"

"*It's our secret, Kevin. But remember what Mr. Norman says about good journalists having a tough hide and a tender heart. That's why you did such a good job with those two obituaries.*" *Again her voice had a pleased sound to it. Kevin wrapped the coils of the phone cord around his finger and then unwound them during the long pause.*

"*I guess you're right,*" *Kevin admitted.* "*I don't know, though, how I feel about these deaths. As long as I'm writing about them it's just an article assignment. But then the reality of it comes crashing in, and I don't know how to deal with it.*" Good grief, what am I doing spilling my guts to you? *Kevin thought.* I'd really like to talk about my confused feelings about you. "*Got any ideas how to cover Traci's death?*" *Kevin found himself asking.* That's right, get back to writing rather than feeling.

"*I guess it all depends on what Mr. Norman says. For acting like such a rebel, he's sure playing this one straight.*"

"*Well, the newspaper and TV keep downplaying the murder angle. But we all know what the boy and his mother told me—slit throat and cross carved into her chest,*" *Kevin observed.*

147

"So do you think there's some kind of cover-up?"

"I don't know, Lori. But it may be that the police don't want a bunch of crazies confessing just to get publicity. So if someone is caught who knows more than just the newspaper and TV reports, then he or she is a more believable suspect."

"So you're saying that we're sitting on details to one of the biggest stories in Lakeshore's history—and we've got to keep sitting on it."

"Sure looks like it."

Another long pause found Kevin twisting the phone cord again until Lori broke the silence.

"Do you ever wonder where people go when they die?" Lori asked.

"Heaven or hell, I guess." One part of Kevin wanted to hang up and go to bed, but another part was intrigued to discover that Lori not only had a physical side—that had been wonderfully transformed over the summer—but an interesting mental and spiritual side. "What do you think?" Kevin asked to keep the conversation going.

"I don't really know if I believe in heaven or hell. Kathy seems to think that we come back in some different form. Maybe that's true. In science class Mr. Collins talked about how we can't destroy energy and matter. So maybe we do just convert into some new energy form."

"Yeah, I remember that," Kevin answered. "He talked about that in an after-school Bible study. He said that when Jesus rose from the dead, he then had a multidimensional body—so he could still eat and be touched, but he could disappear and walk through walls whenever he wanted to."

"So," Lori asked, "do you think that we'll have those kinds of bodies after we die?"

The words after we die *jarred Kevin. Even with all the talk about death, he'd never really thought about his own death. "Ah . . . yeah, I believe we do . . . but I guess I haven't thought a lot about it."*

Before Kevin realized it, the grandfather clock in the entryway was striking twelve o'clock.

149

"Yikes, Lori, I need to get some sleep. It . . . it was good talking with you."

"Yeah, I feel a lot better than I did an hour ago."

"Yeah, me too."

"Well, I guess I better hang up."

"Yeah, me too."

"Well, see you tomorrow."

"Yeah, see ya."

"Bye."

"Bye."

The silent hallways and stunned students standing in small groups were becoming a familiar part of Lakeshore High School. But this time it appeared that Mr. Coldwater had taken the Sentinel's *editorial to heart. Hand-printed signs instructed students to report to the auditorium rather than homeroom at eight o'clock.*

The principal nervously tapped the stage microphone, cleared his throat, and began reading from a four-by-six card: "As you've probably heard by now, Lakeshore High School has tragically lost another student. Friday afternoon Traci Yamagishi was found dead in the field just north of the school. While there are a lot of rumors circulating about the cause of death, I can only tell you what the police have released to the news media. Her death is considered suspicious, and police patrols around the school have been increased.

"Dr. Cooper from Lakeshore Mental Health Center will speak with us briefly about death and the grieving process, and then you'll each go to your regular first-hour class, where a counselor will lead a discussion about your feelings concerning these three recent deaths."

Kevin jotted down notes as Dr. Cooper spoke.

"Hey, Kevin," a familiar voice called as he was exiting the auditorium. He eagerly swung around.

"Oh . . . hi, Kathy."

"You look disappointed—expecting Lori?" Kathy joked. "Wanna know my suspect?"

"Shhhh," Kevin tried to whisper forcefully. "Mr. Norman said to put a lid on it until he talked with us."

"Come on, Kevin. There's no lid big enough for this news. You headed for Norman's office? I'll talk while we walk. Remember how I said I could call up the complete list of what books a person has checked out? Look at this! I ran it this weekend just to confirm my hunch. Jake Stone has checked out every book on the occult and witchcraft in the library. Care to guess the book he currently has out? Satanic Rites and Rituals! It's a virtual 'how-to' on human sacrifice."

"And that's proof?"

"But wait, there's more. Jake asked me this summer if the library had 'Faces of Death'—that really graphic video with people actually being eaten by alligators and electrocuted and stuff. Anyway, I checked with Nate, and he discovered that Jake has rented all four volumes and never once rewound them."

"Not rewinding videos—now there's a capital offense!" Kevin mocked. "And isn't there some kind of law that makes it illegal to go snooping around in people's video rental records?"

"It's called the Video Privacy Protection Act of 1988, and it doesn't apply to criminal investigations," Kathy answered with an air of authority.

"Excuse me, Ms. Future Investigative Reporter."

151

"I'm serious, Kevin. This guy's a logical suspect."

"You haven't told anybody your theory, have you?"

"Just a couple friends."

Kevin rolled his eyes in despair as they entered the journalism office.

"Hey, it looks like the Letters-to-the-Editor box is full!" Kathy announced as she opened the box and began reading letters out loud: "Why can't we have pizza more than once a week?" "Why can't freshmen go to the junior-senior dances?" "Is there any truth to the rumor that the pool is polluted?" Suddenly Kathy stopped reading and began to tremble.

"What's wrong?" Kevin asked with concern.

Kathy just stood there holding a cutout section of last week's Sentinel, *her face white.*

"What is it, Kathy?" Kevin asked more forcefully. He pulled the picture from her hand. It was a photo of the Sentinel *staff. What looked like two knife cuts made a cross through Kathy's heart.*

13
Where Do You Go after You Die?

Of the top-ten questions teens asked in my survey, six related to the number-one question: **"Is there really life after death?"** The number-two question was, **"Do you come back as someone or something else?"** **"Where do you go when you die?"** ranked sixth, followed by **"Are you able to come back as a ghost and haunt people?"** **"What is heaven like?"** and **"What is hell like?"**

Other questions included:

"Do you get a second chance at life after you die?"

"Am I going to be alone when I die?"

"Do you go back to where you were happiest?"

"Is everything after death hunky-dory?"

"What kind of research is being done on this?"

"Is there any evidence of life after death?"

"Can you believe in a lot of stuff dealing with death such as reincarnation, ghosts, life after death, etc.? And if you do believe in these things, aren't you just afraid to deal with death?"

In the next eight chapters we'll try to provide some answers to those questions as we examine near-death experiences, ghosts, communication with the dead, reincarnation, heaven and hell, and finally eternal life. The first theory about life after death is:

⑭ The Big Nothing

Two students wrote:

"I don't believe in God, so I don't believe in heaven or hell, but I'm wondering where do I go?"

"Is there a heaven or hell or are we just blacked out for eternity?"

The position that atheists and humanists take is summed up in the question "Once you're dead, you're dead, right?" Those who believe that our lives are nothing more than highly evolved protoplasm reject the idea of an eternal soul.

So according to this theory, we *do* simply "rot in the ground" with absolutely no awareness or consciousness. After death there is simply nothing, nonexistence, nonbeing, zero, zip. We're no different from a dead flower or a flattened raccoon along the road.

Atheists, humanists, and evolutionists, however, have a difficult time explaining how this "mere mass of cells" can create, dream, plan, design, communicate facts and ideas, and experience emotions such as love and hate, joy and sorrow.

The majority of people do believe that there is something—a soul, a spirit, an image of God, an "essence"—that lives within this hundred-or-so-pound blob of protoplasm we call our body. And the majority of people believe that whatever it is will live for eternity. *Where* it lives is the subject of the next few chapters.

14

Can Your Soul Leave Your Body before You're Dead?

I opened my eyes and looked around as I floated in the cool, eerie silence of Cadillac Lake. I couldn't feel any pain—or anything else—as I mentally checked myself out. *I'll just sit up and rest a bit,* I thought.

Nothing happened.

Well, it's just like a football tackle when you have to wait to get your breath back. After a moment I put every ounce of strength and mental energy into lifting my head out of the water. Again, nothing!

I strained to turn my head so I could gasp for air, but the surface of the lake always seemed just a quarter-inch away from my mouth!

God, I need air! Come on, don't panic. I'll just wait for Mom or my brother to see me and pull me out, and I'll be OK.

Moments before, the sun had shown brightly on the sparkling lake. I was home from college for summer vacation and had been enjoying the laughter and good times with my family at our lakeside cottage in Michigan. I had planned to swim underwater out to the raft to give my mom, brother, and two sisters, who were sunbathing, a good scare. I sprinted to the end of the dock and jumped off at a flat speed dive.

Instantly, my head smashed into something solid. I remember thinking, *This is just like the cartoons where Sylvester is chasing Tweety Bird on skis, and suddenly there's this telephone pole in the middle of the lake. POW!* The skis keep going, but the poor cat slithers down the pole into the water.

Come on, Mom! Notice me! I'm running out of air! I waited and waited. Gradually the sandy lake bottom began turning gray. My lungs felt as if they were being crushed by some invisible vise.

I tried to fight panic as I remembered my lifeguard training. If I passed out, I wouldn't be able to hold my breath any longer. My lungs would begin to fill with water, and I'd be gone. My whole body felt as if it was going to explode with the pounding pressure in my chest.

Lord, I guess this is it, I prayed. *I guess I'm going home. But what makes me deserve heaven? What have I ever done? I've never really shared my faith with the guys in the dorm or the people at work. God, I've failed you.*

But then I sensed God saying, "Don't worry, you're my child." My body began to relax as I felt this beautiful peace and joy. And unbelievable, powerful love seemed to push the pain out of my chest and fill my whole body. Everything had now turned black, and yet there was a feeling that Christ was right beside me. And then, a blinding light as I struggled to open my eyes.

Mike Carlton's story is incredible! According to the paramedics who revived my friend, he had been in the water long enough for severe brain damage. The doctors who treated him said his broken neck should have caused permanent paralysis.

But Mike walked out of the hospital in perfect physical and mental health in just two weeks. Mike, who is now a pastor, believes his faith in God brought him through this close call with death.

Mike's not alone in this experience. Thousands of people come within a breath of death each year, and one-fifth of those resuscitated report some kind of sneak preview of the afterlife!

Can people be brought back from the dead? Medical science defines death as (1) the absence of clinically detectable vital signs, (2) the absence of brain-wave activity, and (3) the irreversible loss of vital functions. Because no one has come back from death as defined this way (with the exception of Jesus Christ and those he raised from the dead), we are talking about *near-death experiences* (NDEs) here.

Many NDEs have several things in common:

1. The sensation of leaving one's body
2. Passing through a dark tunnel
3. Seeing a bright light
4. A sense of love and peace
5. Seeing one's life in review
6. Meeting friends and relatives who have died
7. Making a painful decision to return to earthly life or disappointment at being revived.

Not everyone has all of these experiences, and NDEs aren't limited to these common experiences. Some have reported "floating in a blue bubble," "being held by a giant hand," "straddling a beam of light and touring the universe," and seeing "cities of gold."

And not all of the NDEs are pleasant experiences. Some report "being horrified by nude, zombielike people," and many report "a lake of fire" and the "smell of burning sulphur." One of the ICU nurses we met in chapter 6 reports an unusual case. A thirty-two-year-old woman began bleeding uncontrollably, lost all blood pressure, and went into a coma during a difficult childbirth. While she was being resuscitated, she later reported, she saw her doctor playing cards with a red creature with horns. "They were gambling for my soul," she suggested. The doctor won.

Some researchers believe that there are many more negative experiences than reported for many reasons: the experience is so frightening that the patients block out the memory; they're ashamed to admit that they saw hell rather than heaven; or they fear people will think they're crazy.

But NDEs are nothing new! Ancient Egyptians created these near-death experiences by sealing candidates in mummy coffins for eight minutes as an initiation rite for priests of Osiris and would-be pharaohs. (Archeologists speculate that many slaves died while cult members tried to determine the exact time that one could survive without oxygen and still be revived.) *The Egyptian Book of the Dead* documents these experiments and includes candidates' descriptions of journeys down dark tunnels opening up to bright lights. *The Tibetan Book of the Dead* and *The Aztec Song of the Dead* describe similar phenomena.

Is there proof that people have out-of-body experiences?

Raymond Moody, a medical doctor, was one of the first to attempt to scientifically study NDEs. His two best-selling books, *Life after Life* and *Reflections on Life after Life,* were based on interviews with 150 patients who had close calls with death.

But scientifically verifying NDEs is impossible. In the first place, the studies are based on an extremely limited number of cases. Second, because of patient confidentiality, there is no way to know if the patient is a reliable witness. Is he or she a truthful, mentally stable person? (I'm convinced that Mike Carlton is such a person.) Or has he or she also seen UFOs, the Loch Ness monster, or Elvis recently? Third, the only proof is the patient's subjective memory of a personal experience. There are no other witnesses to verify that this experience did indeed occur. And we all know how stories can become exaggerated after many tellings.

159

Possible Explanations

Russel Noyes of the University of Iowa believes that the sensation of leaving one's body is caused by "transient depersonalizations." In other words, people experiencing near-death events become emotionally detached from their bodies. This allows them to handle a situation without panic and to initiate life-saving measures. Sigmund Freud, the famous psychiatrist, first held this theory, claiming that "our own death is indeed unimaginable and whenever we make an attempt to imagine it, we can perceive that we really survive as spectators." [1]

Similar phenomena are "autoscopic hallucinations," in which people see mirror images of themselves when they suffer from brain tumors, strokes, or migraine headaches. One out of fifty people have experienced these, including President Abraham Lincoln during a bout with migraines.

How does it feel to be out of your body?

But "transient depersonalization" and "autoscopic hallucinations" can't explain away every out-of-body experience. The first scientific report appeared in an 1889 issue of the *St. Louis Medical and Surgical Journal,* where a medical doctor fell into a coma, lost all signs of life, and was pronounced dead by another doctor, S. H. Raynes. After reviving, the doctor reported that while apparently dead, his "non-physical body resembled that of a jellyfish . . . and that his body passed through those of others in the room without contact."[2]

More recently, Michael Sabom, a cardiologist, discovered that thirty-two of his patients claim to have actually left their bodies and watched their own resuscitation. While these patients were not medically trained, each person accurately and with great detail could describe the intricate procedures performed on them while they were apparently unconscious.

Can you see other dead people when you're dead?

People who have near-death experiences also seem to know other things that they shouldn't humanly know. In 1926 Sir William Barrett's book *Deathbed Visions* reported people who were critically ill and so had not been told of a loved one's recent death. And yet when they "returned from death," they described meeting that loved one "on the other side." Many similar stories of talking with dead friends and relatives have been told in recent books and articles.

Do you really travel through a dark tunnel when you die?

The sensation of passing through a dark tunnel can be caused by oxygen loss (hypoxia). Dr. Marshall Goldberg has documented near-drownings (like Mike Carlton's) where patients saw darkness, then a bright light. But Dr. Melvin Morse, author of *Closer to the Light,* claims that many of his patients had adequate oxygen while experiencing NDEs.

One's "life in review" can be explained by brain activity. Under stress or grief the hypothalamus in the brain will signal the pituitary to secrete the hormone ACTH, which has been found to cause one's life to flash before one's eyes—either from infancy to present, or in reverse motion from most recent to early life.

The most dramatic proof that NDEs can be caused by brain activity was documented by Wilder Penfield, known as the father of neurosurgery. In the 1930s Penfield discovered that poking the right temporal lobe of the brain (just above the right ear) produced out-of-body experiences. Since the brain has no feeling, Penfield conducted these experiments with patients wide-awake! Patients spoke of leaving their bodies or being "half in and half out." They also reported "seeing God," hearing beautiful music, seeing dead friends and relatives, and "seeing their life flash before them."

Dr. Karlis Osis thought perhaps these NDEs were the "product of a sick or defective brain," but his research reveals that "the clearer the patient's mind, the more strong this experience was."[3] When he tried to explain the experiences with drugs or high fevers, he made some other interesting discoveries. Of those having NDEs, only one in five were taking drugs, and one in ten had medical conditions (such as brain tumors) that might possibly cause hallucinations; fewer than one in ten had high fevers.

Does your entire life really flash before your eyes?

While many near-death experiences can be explained away physically or medically, there are some cases that seem to have no such explanation. But do these unsolved mysteries prove there is life after death? I don't think so. Here's why:

1. If NDEs are a sneak preview of the afterlife, they should present a fairly similar picture. While there are many people who do see dark tunnels, bright lights, and feel intense love, there are many others who see things as diverse as blue bubbles, zombies, giant hands, and lakes of fire.

2. If NDEs are a sneak preview of the afterlife, they should reveal the same divine presence. However, NDEs

seem to be based on one's religious and cultural background. Protestants see Christ. Catholics tend to see Christ, Mary, or other saints. Hindus see Lord Krishna. Atheists see bright lights or feel great love. Daniel Goleman, who studied NDEs in the United States and India, reports that "no Christian patient saw a Hindu deity, and no Hindu saw Jesus." [4]

Don't out-of-body experiences prove there's life after death?

Many NDEs also contradict the Bible's teaching of the afterlife. For instance, Satan is not the red creature with horns that the bleeding woman reported, but an "angel of light," according to Scripture (2 Corinthians 11:14).

For the person who has lived through a brush with death, the experience is real—whether it can be explained away by modern science or not. But using it to prove anything about the afterlife just isn't possible.

15

Are There Really Such Things as Ghosts?

Before I answer that question, let me say that there really are such things as vampires and werewolves, according to Dr. David Dolphin of the University of British Columbia in a report to the American Association for the Advancement of Science.[1]

Dolphin has been studying a rare disease known as *porphyria,* which may have prompted folktales of werewolves and vampires. Porphyria victims' bodies are unable to produce heme, the red pigment in blood hemoglobin.

"It is our contention that blood-drinking vampires were in fact victims of porphyria, trying to alleviate the symptoms of their dreaded disease," Dolphin writes.

Without heme the skin becomes extremely sensitive to sunlight. "Exposure to even mild sunlight can be devastating," according to Dolphin. Thus all the creature-of-the-night tales.

But what about the transformation from mild-mannered man to hairy creature? Sunlight causes skin sores that can so deform hands that they slowly begin to resemble paws. Lips and gums become taut, exposing the teeth. And to complete the werewolf look, the body tries to protect itself from light by increased hair growth.

OK, Doc, but what about the stories of repelling vampires and werewolves with garlic? Dolphin's research shows that, for some reason, porphyria victims are also violently allergic to the spaghetti seasoning.

In the same way, the stories of ghosts can often be explained as unusual—but explainable—phenomena that get exaggerated in the retelling.

For instance, one of the most publicized "hauntings" was *The Amityville Horror.* In 1974 twenty-four-year-old Ronald DeFeo shot his parents, two brothers, and two sisters to death in their home in Amityville, Long Island. During the trial DeFeo claimed that voices in the house had been telling him to kill his family. Those are facts recorded in court documents.

Are you able to come back as a ghost and haunt people?

One year later the scene of the crime was purchased by George and Kathy Lutz. That too is a verified fact. One month later the Lutzes suddenly moved out, claiming to be tormented by "strange voices seeming to come from within themselves [and] of a power charge which actually lifted Mrs. Lutz off her feet toward a closet behind which was a room not noted on any blueprints."[2]

The couple hired a professional writer, Jay Anson, to ghostwrite (no pun intended) an account of their month of horror in the house.

The book, which allegedly reports "the true story" of "diabolical voices, visions of the mass murderer, and everything from a plague of flies to a plague of demons," became a best-selling book in 1977. It was transformed into a box-office success that exaggerated the events of the book.

Every independent investigation of the case found that the evidence for the sensational events of the book and movie depended solely on the word of the Lutzes. Even the writer, Jay Anson, admitted that he didn't know what was real or fiction—he simply wrote what the Lutzes told him. And the present owners of the famous house report no strange experiences.

Frank Podmore, a pioneer in psychic research, discovered in his investigations that firsthand accounts written by the people who had actually been there tell of strange noises, broken objects, and relatively "unspectacular events." Several months later, however, those same people told much more "impressive" stories. And secondhand accounts—from people who had heard about the haunting, but not actually witnessed it—were even more interesting.

So exaggeration in the retelling may explain some ghostly appearances. But psychiatrist and author Paul Meier has another theory. He tells the story of a five-year-old girl whose father, as he was being carried away to an ambulance after a heart attack, promised, "Don't worry, dear—I'll be back." The girl later reported that the ghost of her dead father came back each night to tuck her into bed.

Meier claims that after intensive therapy and tranquilizers the "ghost" disappeared. He also points out that "voices" always disappear when antipsychotic medication is prescribed. "Deceased 'spirits' must really hate that stuff!" he adds.

Can ghosts hurt you?

The psychiatrist believes that virtually all "ghosts" are auditory or visual hallucinations. "About 3 percent of the American population is psychotic or borderline psychotic at any one time. Many of these persons really believe they communicate with the dead, 'hearing' voices of deceased loved ones as clearly as if they were audible."[3]

Various "proofs" for the existence of ghosts have been offered, such as "ghost photography" (which in virtually every case has turned out to be film defects or deliberate double exposures) and "ghost recordings" (muffled, distorted recordings that only the person doing the recording can seem to understand). Again, every "proof" has been explained away as innocent or deliberate fraud.

Ghost stories, then, seem to fall into three categories:

1. Actual unusual events that become exaggerated in the retelling (e.g., vampires and werewolves)

2. Events that are made up for fame or financial gain (e.g., *The Amityville Horror* and "ghost photos")

For instance, one fourteen-year-old wrote on my survey, **"My brother and my cousin said they have seen a ghost with red eyes. They seemed so serious and really think they did."** I'll bet a bag of Oreos that these guys have become really popular around the youth camp bonfire with their "real" ghost story. Even people who "see" Elvis get national coverage.

Isn't there proof that ghosts do exist?

3. Events that seem very real to the person, but can be explained by extreme grief over the deceased person or by chemical imbalances in the brain

Perhaps it is our overwhelming desire for immortality that makes some of us want to believe in ghosts. And there is a way for our "spirit" to live forever. We'll talk about it in chapters 19 and 21.

16
Can You Talk to the Dead?

Not even AT&T can "reach out and touch someone" like the California realtor who operates "Heaven's Union."

For just forty bucks (sorry, no discounts after eleven o'clock or on weekends) you can send a message to your favorite person beyond the pearly gates. The "operators" are terminally ill patients who are given your message just before their own death.

How can you be sure you don't get a wrong number or a really warm area code? According to Heaven's Union, "Messengers are fully aware of their situation and have had time to repent of past mistakes."

Can you communicate with the dead? If you want to be absolutely sure your call is completed as dialed, "Priority Service" is offered. For just $125 the same message will be carried by three dying patients. (Sorry, no collect calls!)

While this is one of the few services that promise to send a message *to* the dead, mediums, spiritualists, and witch doctors have been claiming to receive messages *from* the dead for centuries.

One of the most famous cases is found, strangely enough, in the Bible, at a time when claiming to contact the dead was punishable with one's own death (Exodus

22:18; Deuteronomy 18:9-14). King Saul, who had lost favor with God, was desperate for advice on how to defeat the Philistines (who were still pretty steamed after David killed their local folk hero Goliath).

Saul then instructed his aides to try to find a medium so that he could ask her what to do, and they found one at Endor. Saul disguised himself by wearing ordinary clothing instead of his royal robes. He went to the woman's home at night, accompanied by two of his men.

"I've got to talk to a dead man," he pleaded. "Will you bring his spirit up?"

"Are you trying to get me killed?" the woman demanded. "You know that Saul has had all the mediums and fortune-tellers executed. You are spying on me."

But Saul took a solemn oath that he wouldn't betray her.

Finally the woman said, "Well, whom do you want me to bring up?"

"Bring me Samuel," Saul replied.

When the woman saw Samuel, she screamed, "You've deceived me! You are Saul!"

"Don't be frightened!" the king told her. "What do you see?"

"I see a specter coming up out of the earth," she said.

"What does he look like?"

"He is an old man wrapped in a robe."

Saul realized that it was Samuel and bowed low before him.

"Why have you disturbed me by bringing me back?" Samuel asked Saul.

"Because I am in deep trouble," he replied. "The Philistines are at war with us, and God has left me and won't reply by prophets or dreams; so I have called for you to ask you what to do."

But Samuel replied, "Why ask me if the Lord has left you and has become your enemy? He has done just as he said he would and has taken the kingdom from you and given it to your rival, David. All this has come upon you because you did not obey the Lord's instructions when he was so angry with Amalek. What's more, the entire Israeli army will be routed and destroyed by the Philistines tomorrow, and you and your sons will be here with me." (1 Samuel 28:7-19)

Was this authentic communication with the dead?

Bible commentator Adam Clark believes that it was an "angel of God" who brought the prophecy of Saul's own death.

Another Bible scholar, Matthew Henry, believes that it was a satanic manifestation.

Psychic investigator and stage magician Danny Korem has the most interesting theory. The word translated "medium" in *The Living Bible* is *oboth* in the original Hebrew. Some versions translate the word "one with a familiar spirit," but at the time of the writing, the word meant "ventriloquist." Korem speculates that the witch of Endor was nothing more than a clever voice-thrower and Saul a real dummy.

Remember, Saul never sees "Samuel." The medium describes what she sees as "an old man wrapped in a robe," which at the time could have described any male over fifty! And Korem believes that her prediction is simply a calculated guess or self-fulfilling prophecy.

Whatever the explanation, there isn't sufficient proof to claim that Samuel really did come back from the dead.

Those who are determined to show that the Bible

proves the reality of contact with the dead also turn to the New Testament.

"There was a certain rich man," Jesus said, "who was splendidly clothed and lived each day in mirth and luxury. One day Lazarus, a diseased beggar, was laid at his door. As he lay there longing for scraps from the rich man's table, the dogs would come and lick his open sores. Finally the beggar died and was carried by the angels to be with Abraham in the place of the righteous dead. The rich man also died and was buried, and his soul went into hell. There, in torment, he saw Lazarus in the far distance with Abraham.

"'Father Abraham,' he shouted, 'have some pity! Send Lazarus over here if only to dip the tip of his finger in water and cool my tongue, for I am in anguish in these flames.'

"But Abraham said to him, 'Son, remember that during your lifetime you had everything you wanted, and Lazarus had nothing. So now he is here being comforted and you are in great anguish. And besides, there is a great chasm separating us, and anyone wanting to come to you from here is stopped at its edge; and no one over there can cross to us.'

"Then the rich man said, 'O Father Abraham, then please send him to my father's home—for I have five brothers—to warn them about this place of torment lest they come here when they die.'

"But Abraham said, 'The Scriptures have warned them again and again. Your brothers can read them any time they want to.'

"The rich man replied, 'No, Father Abraham, they won't bother to read them. But if someone is sent to them from the dead, then they will turn from their sins.'

"But Abraham said, 'If they won't listen to Moses and the prophets, they won't listen even though someone rises from the dead.'" (Luke 16:19-31)

First, this is a parable, or an earthly story that reveals an eternal truth—Jesus is not relating an actual event. If we were to take all parables literally, we would all be wearing wool ("The Lost Sheep") with "In God We Trust" stamped on our backsides ("The Lost Coin") while living in a pigpen ("The Prodigal Son").

Second, it seems to imply that communication from the dead to the living is improbable if not impossible. But the living seem to have an unstoppable desire to believe it's possible.

During the middle 1800s, "spiritism" was popularized by the famous Fox sisters of Rochester, New York. The women claimed that a murdered peddler was communicating to them by rapping (which at that time meant tapping sounds, not to be confused with a modern musical style). Their nationwide fame turned out to be a "bum rap" when one of the psychic sisters confessed that she made the sounds by deliberately cracking her knee joints.

Harry Houdini, the famous escape artist, became interested in the still-popular spiritism of the turn of the century while trying to contact his deceased mother. He continued his study of psychic phenomena after reading *Revelations of a Spirit Medium*. The unnamed author revealed how he became interested in spiritism and tried to develop his own psychic powers, only to discover it was all a fake. The book revealed how mediums could slip in and out of knotted ropes and escape from "spirit cabinets" to create their spirit manifestations.

And thus Houdini's career turned to escapes, as well as duplicating any effect that any medium allegedly accomplished through spirits. In each town, Houdini would challenge local psychics to perform their "manifestations" on stage, and then he would duplicate them through completely natural means.

Scientific American magazine used Houdini as a judge in a five-thousand-dollar challenge. The magazine promised half the money to the first medium who could prove a case of spirit phenomena such as table tipping or "spirit writing." The second half would go to any medium who could prove communication with the dead. No one claimed the prize money.

Houdini continued to search for authentic communication and manifestations from the dead, but he never found any. He also promised to send a message back from the other side after his death if at all possible. Bess Houdini offered ten thousand dollars to any medium who could reveal a ten-word message her husband had promised to send back from the dead. So on each anniversary of the master magician's death—Halloween night—seances have been held to receive a message from Harry Houdini. He has never phoned home.

Can you contact the dead through a seance?

Science and Invention magazine offered twenty thousand dollars for any trick or phenomenon that stage magician John Dunniger couldn't reproduce by ordinary means. No one claimed that prize either.

Ouija boards have become a popular method of communicating with the dead and peeking into the future—especially at junior-high sleep-overs. A triangular pointer called a planchette supposedly glides across a board printed with an alphabet, "Yes," "No," and "Good-bye." But what force guides the planchette to spell out messages from beyond?

Isaac Fuld, who created and patented the game, admitted the mobilizing force was simply "involuntary muscle actions," although he did suggest the possibility that "some other agency" spelled out the messages. Obviously a shrewd marketing ploy![1]

Dr. Paul Meier, a Christian psychiatrist, believes that any results obtained from Ouija boards are either by "trickery, luck, or subconscious ideomotor action."[2] Danny Korem, the psychic investigator mentioned earlier, claims that he has not uncovered one Ouija-board story that can't be explained by subconscious movement of the planchette.

And so there appear to be no authentic, verified contacts with the dead that can't be explained away by subconscious forces or deliberate trickery.

But there is real danger in self-deception. As Sergeant Custer revealed in chapter 7, Ouija boards and books about the occult can lead teens and adults into spiritual darkness. Many Christians believe that using an Ouija board can open a person up to satanic influences. The Bible explicitly forbids occult practices, such as attempting to talk with the dead (Leviticus 20:27; Deuteronomy 18:11-12; 1 Chronicles 10:13-14; Isaiah 8:19), trying to peek into the future with tarot cards or horoscopes (Leviticus 19:26, 31; 20:6), or witchcraft and sorcery (Exodus 22:18; 1 Samuel 15:23; 2 Chronicles 33:6; Malachi 3:5; Matthew 24:24; Acts 19:17-20; Galatians 5:19-21).

17

Do You Really Come Back as Someone Else?

Rob Holt* was . . . well, very, very different. The high school student claimed to be an extraterrestrial. He always wore cotton in his ears to filter out the "earth frequencies," which he claimed were higher pitched than those of his native planet.

And Rob refused to participate in swimming during phys ed since his "high-voltage energy field" would turn us all into boiled lobster, he said, if he got into the pool with us mere humans.

But the biggest difference was his god, Kosgro McOrlo Excelsior. He, she, or it lived in a gold gift box in Rob's locker. And for just twenty-five cents, classmates could take a peek at this god in a box.

I've lost touch with this unique student who most of us thought had lost touch with reality. Was Rob really crazy? There are three possibilities:

1. *Rob was no alien—and he knew it.* The whole Kosgro McOrlo Excelsior routine was a scam to rip off students' lunch money. If so, instead of a court-appointed psychiatrist, Rob deserved an Oscar for Best Portrayal of an Alien by a High-School Student—or at least a warning from the Better Business Bureau.

*(not his real name)

2. *Rob was no alien—but he really thought he was.* In this case, inpatient treatment at the state mental hospital was probably in order.

3. *Rob really* was *an alien.* The rest of us were merely ignorant earthlings who were unaware of Rob's remarkable powers.

Simply the fact that something is hard to believe doesn't make it false. We've all experienced events that cause us to exclaim, "You're not gonna believe what happened!" Say, for instance, we sink a basketball from half court. How can others know that it's true? There are several questions that relate to both Rob and the incredible basket:

1. Is Rob a credible person? Can we believe what he says? Can people believe us when we say we sank a basketball from half court?

2. Are Rob's stories consistent with each other? Are they consistent with other stories of extraterrestrials? In the case of the basketball shot, do we tell the same story, with the same details each time?

3. Can other people prove Rob's story? Are there reliable eyewitnesses to his supernatural powers? Were our friends or the coach watching when we sank the basket?

4. Does Rob's "history" and "observations" of the universe agree with historical or scientific evidence? Our basket can't be "scientifically" proven, since that would demand that we could readily repeat the feat (we probably can't). But we could have "historical" proof (eyewitnesses, videotape, or an article in the school paper) verifying that it did happen at one point in time. Others can go to the school and see the basketball hoop and ball.

If there are major flaws in Rob's story, then it's doubtful that Rob is really a space-traveling follower of Kosgro McOrlo Excelsior. But if his story stands up to reasonable investigation, then we need to give it serious consideration.

The same kind of questions need to be asked of those who believe in reincarnation.

A good number of people do believe in reincarnation—two-thirds of the world's population, and, according to a 1981 Gallup poll, thirty-eight million Americans.

177

Reincarnation teaches that our souls are a part of the essence of God and that we come back to earth in different forms until we reach the highest level of "god-ness" or "universal consciousness," or "Nirvana."

Do you really come back as someone else?

Hinduism teaches that we get a brand-new body with each cycle. Buddhists, however, believe that each new body is made up of the same kind of *skandhas,* which, loosely translated, means "goo." The majority of reincarnationists—and virtually all ancient believers—hold that humans can be recycled as frogs, trees, or sacred cows.

Americanized reincarnation, however, teaches that humans can only come back as humans. (We'll talk more about this later.)

An important doctrine of reincarnation is *karma*—a cosmic Chutes and Ladders game. This force determines whether we come back as royalty or a rootworm. If we live a good life and learn our lessons well, we will come back at a higher level of society, or *caste.* If we're dirty rotten scoundrels, we slide down a few notches.

Are Reincarnationists Credible People? Can We Believe What They Say?

American reincarnationists include doctors; lawyers; college professors from such universities as Cambridge, Harvard, and Yale; politicians; and theologians. So we're not talking about just people with shaved heads, wearing white sheets and selling flowers in airports.

Reincarnation in America has become increasingly popular due to the best-selling books by Edgar Cayce, "the father of modern reincarnation," and more recently, those by actress/dancer Shirley MacLaine, *Out on a Limb* and *Dancing in the Light.*

Are these credible people? We'll discover later that Cayce—a fifth-grade dropout who couldn't read—didn't know much about history. MacLaine claims that under "psychic acupuncture" she is able to talk to animals, trees, and her "higher self." If students in your class started talking about these things, they'd find themselves talking to the school psychologist.

MacLaine, if she is credible, should also be accurate—since she is in touch with "infinite wisdom." She argues that Jesus taught reincarnation by preaching, "As you sow, so shall you reap." There are two fallacies to that argument: First, the passage refers to reaping what we sow in this life—not in some future life. And second, Jesus never said it. It was the apostle Paul (Galatians 6:7).

MacLaine also alleges that the theory of reincarnation was recorded in the Bible, but that the religious Council of Nicea in A.D. 553 deleted all mention of it. Again, she's in error. The Council of Nicea met in A.D. 325 and dealt with Origen's idea that souls were formed before conception. At issue was the creation of the soul, not reincarnation—and removal of Scripture portions was never discussed.

Such serious errors tend to undermine MacLaine's credibility.

John Van Auken, author of *Born Again . . . and Again,* stretches his credibility thread thin when he speaks of mythological animals, such as centaurs (half horse/half man), satyrs (half goat/half man), sphinxes (half lion/half man), and mermaids and mermen, as real beings that roamed the early earth.

Are these people credible witnesses? You decide. But according to MacLaine, credibility is irrelevant! Read on.

Can Reincarnationists Prove Their Stories? Are There Reliable Eyewitnesses to the Reincarnation?

Like the out-of-body experiences we discussed in chapter 14, reincarnation experiences are impossible to verify since there are absolutely no outside witnesses to verify an individual's story.

Modern reincarnationists try to avoid any judgment or analysis of their claims because, as MacLaine writes, "truth and reality are relative, existing only in the mind. . . . Reality is what each of us decides it is."

In other words, because Rob believes Kosgro McOrlo Excelsior exists, it therefore exists. And he, she, or it is just as real as this word processor I'm typing on—at least according to MacLaine. Then again, she wouldn't admit that this Zenith laptop computer is real because "the cosmos [is] nothing but consciousness. The universe and God itself might just be one giant, collective thought."[1]

So according to MacLaine, the questions of "proof" and "reliability" are irrelevant because there is no such thing as truth or falsehood, good or evil. People have "their own perceptions, their own truth, their own pace, and their own versions of enlightenment. It [is] not possible to judge another's truth."[2]

So are we to believe that Adolph Hitler, who ordered the death of 6 million Jews, and Jeffery Dahmer, who recently tortured, raped, and then ate fifteen young men, were merely misunderstood? According to MacLaine, the answer is yes.

"Tragedy is tragedy because we *perceive* it as such." We choose what happens to us, such as Nazi death camps and Dahmer's freezer, "whether it was a love affair, a death, a lost job, or a disease. We choose to have the experiences in order to learn from them."[3]

On the contrary, Jesus Christ's resurrection (not to be confused with reincarnation), has reliable, verifiable historical evidence. (We'll talk more about this in chapter 18.)

So, while faith is important, I would question any belief that depends completely on the unverifiable testimony of its followers.

Are Reincarnationists' Stories Consistent with Each Other?

As we pointed out about near-death experiences, if they are real, there should be some consistency in the stories. The same test must apply to reincarnation.

Hindu reincarnation is different from the Buddhist version, and the American version contradicts both of the Eastern versions.

When reincarnation came to America, the idea of humans possibly becoming flies or sacred cows just didn't sell. So the system of belief was simply changed to appeal to an American audience: "No, you don't come back as a lower life-form. In fact, you just keep coming back as better and better people." Ralph Waldo Emerson, the famous author and transcendental meditation guru, promoted this idea as "up and onward forevermore!"[4]

However, Edgar Cayce disagreed with Emerson. He saw his past lives as a "constant roller coaster, up and down; now a high priest and virtual ruler of Egypt, then a humble warrior in Troy or a . . . ne'er-do-well scout in colonial America."[5]

Western reincarnationists not only reject the Hindu

Do you really come back as something else? . . . as a fly? . . . as a buffalo?

belief of going backward in the next life, but they also reject the basic force behind reincarnation—karma. As we noted, MacLaine believes we "choose" our next life rather than having karma seal our fate.

There are also great differences of opinion when it comes to whether the reincarnated can know their past lives. Some, like Geddes MacGregor, argue that one cannot know about his or her past lives. "Deprivation of memory [is] essential to new development and growth." [6]

Do you get to pick what you come back as?

Others claim that "inherited memory" or "collective unconsciousness" is remembering the life of some ancestor that has been genetically transmitted rather than an individual remembering his own past.

Others, like Edgar Cayce and Shirley MacLaine, write very specific accounts of their own previous lives. (We'll talk about Cayce's "lives" later.)

The Westernized version of reincarnation rejects two-thirds of the ancient Eastern philosophy with an if-we-don't-agree-we-don't-believe attitude. And, for them, that's fine because there is no truth or falsehood—just personal revelation.

Do Reincarnationists' "History" and "Observations" Agree with Historical or Scientific Evidence?
Twisted Scripture

As I pointed out in *Should a Christian Wear Purple Sweat Socks?* "With over twenty-three thousand verses to choose from, you can find a verse to prove your point on any current controversy." [7] We must read the Bible in its total context—not just pull verses out of context that seem to prove our point.

Shirley MacLaine and other reincarnationists try to make the Bible prove reincarnation, but Hebrews 9:27-28 is quite clear: "And just as it is destined that [a person] die only once, and after that comes judgment, so also Christ died only once as an offering for the sins of many people."

Do people remember who they were in their past life?

Instead of this clear biblical principle, MacLaine and company write of Jesus and his disciples as being born again—and again and again.

They take several verses in the Gospel of John completely out of context:

Jesus replied, "With all the earnestness I possess I tell you this: Unless you are born again, you can never get into the Kingdom of God."

"Born again!" exclaimed Nicodemus. "What do you mean? How can an old man go back into his mother's womb and be born again?"

Jesus replied, "What I am telling you so earnestly is this: Unless one is born of water and the Spirit, he cannot enter the Kingdom of God. Men can only reproduce human life, but the Holy Spirit gives new life from heaven; so don't be surprised at my statement that you must be born again!" (John 3:3-7)

Jesus is specifically speaking against reincarnation when he makes the distinction between physical birth and the new spiritual life. "Men can only reproduce human life," but this rebirth Christ is speaking of is from the Holy Spirit. (We'll talk more about this in chapter 21.)

Another section that reincarnationists like to misinterpret is John 8:57-58, where Jesus is proclaiming his eternal nature as God:

The Jewish leaders: "You aren't even fifty years old—sure, you've seen Abraham!"

Jesus: "The absolute truth is that I was in existence before Abraham was ever born."

At issue is Jesus' timelessness as God. Since Christ was fully God and God has existed for eternity, then it follows that he was alive before Abraham. Proving that Christ is eternal doesn't prove in any way that *we* are!

Does being born again mean being rein-carnated? Reincarnationists also point to Christ's "transfiguration" (Matthew 17:1-5; Mark 9:2-8; Luke 9:28-35), where he meets with Moses and Elijah, as proof of reincarnation. Again, it merely points out that Moses' and Elijah's spirits were very much alive in God's presence (we'll talk about that in chapter 19), but that doesn't prove anything about reincarnation.

Those who try to make the Bible prove reincarnation also point to references of John the Baptist being the reincarnation of the Old Testament prophet Elijah.

His disciples asked, "Why do the Jewish leaders insist Elijah must return before the Messiah comes?"

Jesus replied, "They are right. Elijah must come and set everything in order. And, in fact, he has already come, but he wasn't recognized, and was badly mistreated by many. And I, the Messiah, shall also suffer at their hands."

Then the disciples realized he was speaking of John the Baptist. (Matthew 17:10-13)

Was this messenger of Christ actually Elijah? The archangel Gabriel, who announced his birth, prophesied, "He will be a man of rugged spirit and power *like* Elijah, the prophet of old" (Luke 1:17, italics added). John the Baptist himself denied he was Elijah in John 1:21. Jesus, however, does state, "John appeared, and if you are willing to understand what I mean, he *is* Elijah" (Matthew 11:13-14, italics mine).

If John the Baptist was actually the prophet Elijah, it is such an unusual occurrence that it hardly proves reincarnation. Elijah never died but was flown into the presence of God on "a chariot of fire, drawn by horses of fire . . . carried by a whirlwind" (2 Kings 2:11). John the Baptist was born to an elderly couple who had been unable to have children (Luke 1:5-13). If God can beam a man up into heaven in a fiery chariot, cause a couple past childbearing years to have a baby, and come to earth as a baby born to a virgin (Luke 1:26-35), then it's probably no problem for him to bring back the prophet Elijah as John the Baptist. But to imply that this proves reincarnation *is* a problem.

The apostle Paul was aware that there would "come a time when people won't listen to the truth but will go around looking for teachers who will tell them just what they want to hear. They won't listen to what the Bible says but will blithely follow their own misguided ideas" (2 Timothy 4:3-4).

Can MacLaine and her followers be credible when they distort and take out of context historical documents such as the Bible?

A "Cayce" history

Edgar Cayce, in whom Shirley MacLaine and her medium Kevin Ryerson place so much faith, was far from a faithful historian. The "sleeping prophet," as he was known, fell into trances in which he would recall past lives as his followers would transcribe his observations.

He claims his first life was in Atlantis, the mythical "lost continent." But it was far from mythical to Cayce.

Atlanteans were "not yet in the flesh, were thought-forms, disembodied energy."[8] These sexless thoughts eventually became male and female people who travelled the seas on high-tech hovercrafts at over seven hundred miles per hour. When the dinosaurs became a nuisance, the Atlanteans simply disintegrated them with cosmic ray guns. Where is Atlantis today? According to Cayce, the five islands went to war with nuclear weapons, causing massive earthquakes and tidal waves that buried the land at the bottom of the Atlantic Ocean.

Cayce supposedly went on to live as the high priest Ra-Ta in Egypt, a medicine man in Persia, and the infamous Xeon of Troy, who opened the gates of the city to the Trojan Horse. He then appeared in Judea as Lucius the Cyrene, one of the prophets and teachers noted in the Bible (Acts 13:1).

It would appear that if one continues to get better and better, there wouldn't be far to go after being a biblical prophet. But Cayce claims he came back later to "indulge his sexual appetites" in France and the colony of Virginia as the father of illegitimate children.

Although Cayce's stories are hard to believe, remember that is not sufficient evidence to write them off. But these "Cayce histories" have no historical evidence. Plato wrote of the "lost continent of Atlantis," yet there is no solid historical or archeological evidence for such an advanced civilization. Other Cayce histories are absolutely incorrect. For instance, Cayce claimed that Jesus Christ had previously been Adam and then Enoch. That would be hard to do, since Adam and Enoch were alive at the same time! Cayce also claims to have been Lucius ministering in Judea, when Scripture records him far north in Antioch of Syria.

Can someone with so little accuracy be trusted? You decide.

185

Unscientific theories

Ivan Stevenson, a psychiatrist who served at several universities and hospitals, believes that he has "proof" that reincarnation explains everything from birthmarks to cravings during pregnancy. Stevenson believes that birthmarks are actually scars from previous lives. He claims to have examined more than two hundred cases where gunshot wounds, knife cuts—even beheadings—in other lives have shown up as birthmarks.

He also believes that phobias (fears of heights, water, insects, etc.) are actually memories of past lives when one was killed by falling off a cliff, drowning in a shipwreck, or being bitten by a black widow spider. "Love at first sight" occurs when two people who were lovers in a past life meet in this life. Child prodigies who excel at piano were probably concert pianists in another life, according to the psychiatrist.

Will we have the same scars and problems we had in another life?

Heredity seems to be a much more believable explanation for birthmarks—which are not "scars" at all, but clusters of melanin (the pigment that produces skin color). Fears can be traced easily from earlier experiences, rather than delving into past lives. And chapter 8 of my book *Sex Is Not a Four-Letter Word* provides a more reasonable explanation for love at first sight.

But John McTaggart of Cambridge University believes that heredity does not rule out reincarnation, but actually *supports* the theory. He teaches that eternal souls search for fetuses that are most like their previous bodies. He describes it as a man looking for the right-sized hat to wear. So it is not heredity that creates a certain characteristic or talent; rather, an eternal soul just happened to find a body that suited his or her talents and abilities.

Reincarnationists also try to explain away heredity

with an "electric architect" or "astral body." Harold S. Burr writes of his experiments at Yale in his *Blueprint for Immortality: The Electric Patterns of Life*. Dr. Burr claims these eternal blueprints are the "electrodynamic field" of the "real body" of a person upon which the physical body is built. Hindus speak of "chakras" and Buddhists of "lotus centers," which connect the astral bodies to the physical bodies. Acupuncture (sticking long needles into these points) supposedly brings healing by reconnecting these two bodies.

And so Burr believes that chromosomes and DNA, which control fetal development, are actually controlled by this overriding electrodynamic field.

More Questions?

Reincarnation has been seriously questioned for thousands of years. The early church leader Tertullian argued against reincarnation because it couldn't account for the population explosion of his time. Now, several billion people later, his argument is even more persuasive. Ivan Stevenson suggests that souls are simply being recycled at a faster rate in our century or that more subhuman animals are being reincarnated as humans. (So that's where all the endangered species are going?)

Others ask, Why aren't we more advanced if souls continue to grow closer to this "universal wisdom"? Why do crime rates continue to skyrocket? Why have there been more wars in this century than any other? Reincarnationists like MacLaine would simply argue that there are only "perceptions." The Hiroshima and Nagasaki atomic blasts were only perceptions?

Perhaps our world is growing worse rather than better in part because of the belief in reincarnation. Karma allows the wealthy of India to walk past the homeless with absolutely no sense of social responsibility. To help them out of their wretched existence would be interfering with karma. Better that they learn their lessons and die of starvation quickly with the hope of improving their lot in life the next time around.

188 So instead of leading to a love for others, karma leads to a selfish disregard for other humans. Any good that one does is a self-centered attempt to improve his or her station in the next life. No wonder India, "the land of enlightenment," is one of the poorest countries in the world.

So is reincarnation a credible belief system? Make sure you carefully examine the evidence before you decide.

18
What If This Christianity Stuff Isn't Real?

Jana sat across from me in the youth camp dining hall after all the other teens had left.

"I've got a question for you," she began.

"OK," I said.

"What if this Christianity stuff isn't real? I've got an aunt who's really into the New Age—you know, crystals and channelling—and she really believes in it. I mean, she believes in it more than I believe in Christianity."

"Well, it really doesn't matter that you believe," I responded. Jana stared at me as if she were going into shock. I hurried to explain. "Say, for instance, you believed—absolutely, wholeheartedly, sincerely—that this saltshaker was your ticket to heaven." She continued to stare at me without saying anything. "Would believing it make it true?" I asked.

Aren't there a lot of ways to heaven?

"No," she finally answered.

"So it's not *that* you believe but *what* you believe."

"OK, I can see that. But how can you know that Christianity is the right thing to believe and everything else is wrong? Aren't there a lot of ways to heaven?"

"Jesus doesn't allow any alternate routes to heaven. He declared, 'I am the Way—yes, and the Truth and the Life.

No one can get to the Father [and heaven] except by means of me'" (John 14:6).

"OK, but how can I know that what Jesus said was true?" she continued.

"By asking the same tough questions we asked about reincarnation in yesterday's seminar." And with that we were off on a good discussion using the same questions we asked in the last chapter:

- Are the witnesses credible people? Can we believe what they say?
- Can they prove their stories? Are there reliable eye-witnesses?
- Are the stories consistent with each other?
- Do the reported "history" and "observations" agree with historical and scientific evidence?

In all fairness, we need to apply these very same tests to the belief in a heaven and a hell. If you, like Jana, are seriously questioning whether the biblical account of the afterlife is accurate, it will be worth your time to consider the following evidence.

Keep in mind that simply because something is hard to believe doesn't make it false. And just because something can't be "scientifically proven" doesn't make it untrue. Remember in chapter 17 we discussed how we couldn't prove scientifically that we sank an unbelievable basket from half court. That would demand that we readily repeat the feat.

But we can prove that we made the basket with "historical proof." In the same way, written reports of eyewitnesses are the only way that we know that Julius Caesar ruled the Roman Empire, that the Pilgrims landed at Plymouth Rock, or that President Abraham Lincoln was assassinated.

Are the Writers of the Bible Credible People? Can We Believe What They Say?

Let's begin with Jesus Christ. Is he really the Son of God or is he, as the reincarnationists would argue, simply a very good man? Jesus himself claimed to be God (Mark 9:37; John 12:44; 14:9). He accepted worship (Matthew 14:33; Luke 5:8; John 20:28). He told his followers to pray in his name (John 16:23). He even claimed that he was able to forgive sin (Matthew 9:2-7, 12:8; Mark 2:5-7; Luke 7:47-48).

C. S. Lewis claimed that Jesus couldn't be a good man. He was either Lord, a liar, or a lunatic.

Can we believe the people who wrote the Bible?

I am trying here to prevent anyone saying the really foolish thing that people often say about Him: "I'm ready to accept Jesus as a great moral teacher, but I don't accept His claim to be God." That is the one thing we must not say. A man who was merely a man and said the sort of thing Jesus said would not be a great moral teacher. He would either be a lunatic— on the level with the man who says he is a poached egg—or else he would be the Devil of Hell. You must make your choice. Either this man was, and is, the Son of God; or else a madman or something worse. You can shut Him up for a fool, you can spit at Him and kill Him as a demon; or you can fall at His feet and call Him Lord and God. But let us not come with any patronizing nonsense about His being a great human teacher. He has not left that open to us. He did not intend to.[1]

Some argue, however, that Christ never claimed to be Lord; that later editors slipped these "divine" delusions into the text. But, as we'll discuss later, there are twenty-four thousand ancient portions of the New Testament available for scrutiny. So any later attempt at deception would surely be exposed. It hasn't been! We must accept as fact that Jesus did claim to be God.

Christ's credibility as God can be argued from the prophecies made about him in the Old Testament. God revealed to godly men what would occur hundreds of years into the future. And so, centuries before Christ's birth, the ancient prophets made amazing predictions, which Jesus accurately and precisely fulfilled. But couldn't first-century editors have slipped these prophecies into the writings of the B.C. writers to make it look like Christ fulfilled prophecy?

If they did, they would have surely been exposed when archeologists recently discovered copies of these precise prophecies of Isaiah dating back to 125 B.C. Unless those editors had a flux-capacitor-powered chariot (à la *Back to the Future*'s time machine) this would be impossible!

Let's look at some of those prophecies.[2] Micah (5:2) claimed Christ would be born in Bethlehem, Hosea (11:1) prophesied he would come out of Egypt, and another claimed he would live in Nazareth. "See," the ancient sceptics probably laughed, "Scripture contradicts itself!"

But Jesus was born in *Bethlehem,* smuggled into *Egypt* to avoid the wrath of King Herod, and—once the threat was over—taken to *Nazareth,* where he grew up (Matthew 2).

The prophet Isaiah spoke of his miracles: "And when he comes, he will open the eyes of the blind and unstop the ears of the deaf. The lame man will leap up like a deer, and those who could not speak will shout and sing!" (Isaiah 35:5-6). No mere human could have done the things that history records Jesus doing!

As Christ entered Jerusalem the prophecy of Zechariah was fulfilled: "Rejoice greatly, O my people! Shout with joy! For look—your King is coming! He is the

Righteous One, the Victor! Yet he is lowly, riding on a donkey's colt!" (9:9).

OK, Jesus could have read the prophecy and deliberately planned to "fulfill" this prophecy. But he couldn't have controlled the spontaneous outpouring of praise from children predicted in the book of Psalms (8:2).

Even Christ's betrayal—which would have been hard to deliberately arrange—was foretold by the prophets in exact detail, right down to the exact amount given the betrayer! The prophet Zechariah wrote that thirty pieces of silver would be the price. And he prophesied that the betrayer would return the money. Zechariah even foretold that the betrayer would throw the money on the temple floor and that the thirty pieces would buy a potter's field (11:12-13). Again, remember that these predictions were in print hundreds of years before Christ was born!

His crucifixion—which no one would want to stage—was foretold in graphic detail. The prophet Isaiah spoke of Jesus being beaten, whipped, spat upon, and crucified with thieves (50:6; 53:5, 12). The psalmist wrote of his clothing being gambled over and of his being given vinegar to drink (Psalms 22:15; 69:21). The prophet Amos foretold the darkness that covered the land during the crucifixion (8:9). The psalmist even prophesied Christ's exact words from the cross: "My God, my God, why have you forsaken me" (Psalm 22:1).

Peter Stoner has estimated that the odds against one man fulfilling just eight of these prophecies is one in 100,000,000,000,000,000![3] Stoner helps us visualize 10^{17} (the scientific notation of 10 followed by seventeen zeros). Imagine the state of Texas two feet deep in silver dollars. The odds of a blindfolded man finding a specially marked dollar on the first try are one in 10^{17}.

That's just for accurately fulfilling eight of the sixty prophecies that Christ specifically fulfilled!

Can the Writers of the Bible Prove Their Stories? Are There Reliable Eyewitnesses to the Events Recorded in the Bible?

Let's take the most outrageous, unbelievable claim in Scripture: that Jesus Christ was killed, buried, and yet rose to life again on the third day. Is it a historical fact? Here's what the Bible claims:

> Early on Sunday morning, as the new day was dawning, Mary Magdalene and the other Mary went out to the tomb.
>
> Suddenly there was a great earthquake; for an angel of the Lord came down from heaven and rolled aside the stone and sat on it. His face shone like lightning and his clothing was a brilliant white. The guards shook with fear when they saw him, and fell into a dead faint.
>
> Then the angel spoke to the women. "Don't be frightened!" he said. "I know you are looking for Jesus, who was crucified, but he isn't here! For he has come back to life again, just as he said he would. Come in and see where his body was lying. . . . And now, go quickly and tell his disciples that he has risen from the dead, and that he is going to Galilee to meet them there. That is my message to them."
>
> The women ran from the tomb, badly frightened, but also filled with joy, and rushed to find the disciples to give them the angel's message. And as they were running, suddenly Jesus was there in front of them!
>
> "Good morning!" he said. And they fell to the ground before him, holding his feet and worshiping him. (Matthew 28:1–9)

Has there ever been anyone who has died and come back to life?

Wilbur Smith claims, "The *meaning* of the Resurrection is a theological matter, but the *fact* of the resurrection is a historical matter; the nature of the resurrection body of Jesus may be a mystery, but the fact the body disappeared from the tomb is a matter to be decided upon by historical evidence." [4]

Those who wish to explain away the Resurrection run into an entire road map of dead ends.

Some claim that Christ merely "swooned" on the cross and revived in the tomb. How can they explain that the Roman crucifixion squad, whose sole duty was to kill criminals, declared Jesus dead? Certainly these men, experienced executioners, wouldn't make such a serious mistake. How can they explain that a man bleeding from head, back, wrist, and feet wounds—along with a spear puncture in his side—could possibly revive enough to escape from mummylike burial cloths, push away a thousand-pound rock sealing the tomb, and sneak past armed guards? That requires more faith to believe than that he simply rose from the dead!

Others claim that the disciples stole Christ's body and made up the story of the Resurrection. Scripture says that:

As the women were on the way into the city, some of the Temple police who had been guarding the tomb went to the chief priests and told them what had happened. A meeting of all the Jewish leaders was called, and it was decided to bribe the police to say they had all been asleep when Jesus' disciples came during the night and stole his body.

"If the governor hears about it," the Council promised, "we'll stand up for you and everything will be all right."

So the police accepted the bribe and said what they were told to. Their story spread widely among the Jews, and is still believed by them to this very day. (Matthew 28:11-15)

Again, the theory that Christ's disciples stole his body requires a flying leap of faith. How could disciples who ran into hiding after their leader's arrest suddenly be courageous enough to fight their way through armed guards to steal Christ's body? (Only one of the apostles, John, and a few women had courage enough to show up at Christ's execution.) And how do we explain the fact that these selfish cowards of disciples could go to their death singing the praises of their resurrected Savior, if it was indeed a total hoax?

Others have tried to explain Christ's resurrection by saying that his post-resurrection appearances were merely hallucinations. However, five hundred people are recorded to have seen Jesus after his resurrection.

Amazingly, not one record has been found in ancient writing that rejects the idea of Christ's resurrection. If indeed it was a hoax, the residents of Jerusalem could easily have verified it as false.

Are the Books of the Bible Consistent with Each Other?

Considering that the Bible was written over sixteen hundred years by at least forty different authors on three different continents in three different languages on hundreds of controversial subjects, there is amazing harmony in the text.

There are some minor details that seem to contradict one another. For instance, in the account of Jesus cursing a fruitless fig tree, Matthew records that it died and withered up "immediately" (21:19, NIV), but Mark records it was dead by the "next morning" (11:20-21). There are several other discrepancies in the accounts of Christ's last week on earth.

But if we look at the Bible as a whole, the contradictions account for less than a fraction of one percent. The Bible exceeds Ivory soap's claim of "99.44%" purity!

Do the Bible's "History" and "Observations" Agree with Historical and Scientific Evidence?

Francis Schaeffer, a Christian philosopher and former skeptic, writes:

> Christianity involves history. To say only that is already to have said something remarkable, because it separates the Judeo-Christian worldview from almost all other religious thought. It is rooted in history. Is the history accurate?
>
> The more we understand about the Middle East between 2500 B.C. and A.D. 100, the more confident we can be that the information in the Bible is reliable, even when it speaks about the simple things of time and space.[5]

Josh McDowell has spent years documenting the accuracy of Scripture with historical and archeological evidence. (He actually began his research to discredit the Bible, but became a believer due to his findings!) He points out that "Christianity appeals to the facts of history . . . the most patent and accessible data. Christ is a fact of history as real as any other."[6]

For instance, some scholars scoffed at the idea of Moses writing the first five books of the Old Testament. They claimed that there was no written language at the time. That would certainly undermine the credibility of the Bible! But in 1974 Paolo Matthiae discovered tablets in the region of northeast Syria that predate Moses by one thousand years. The writings at Ebla also confirmed the existence of biblical cities that modern historians had claimed were simply mythical. According to these ancient tablets, Sodom and Gomorrah, as well as other "lost" cities, really did exist!

Some dismiss the Old and New Testaments of the Bible because the "original manuscripts" have long since disappeared; all we have now are handmade copies. (Remember how Shirley MacLaine claimed that references to reincarnation were removed from the Bible in A.D. 553?)

Before 1947 the oldest copies of the Old Testament were dated A.D. 900—thousands of years after they were originally penned. So there would have been plenty of time for mistakes to be made in copying the scrolls. (Remember this was thousands of years before the printing press and the photocopy machine.)

But with the discovery of the Dead Sea Scrolls, copies of the book of Isaiah were found that had been made around 125 B.C.—one thousand years earlier. The A.D. 900 copies were found to be virtual photocopies of the 125 B.C. copies!

So it appears that the Old Testament was accurately transmitted down through the years.

Even more ancient copies of the New Testament are available—twenty-four thousand copies. Sir Frederick Kenyon of the British Museum claims that the time between the original writings and the earliest-dated copies of New Testament books is "so small as to be in fact negligible." [7]

Compare that with other ancient literature. There are only ten copies of the writings of the Caesar who ruled from 100–44 B.C., and those are dated one thousand years after the originals were written. There are only seven ancient copies of Plato's writings (427–347 B.C.), but the earliest copies are twelve hundred years after the original writing. Aristotle (384–322 B.C.) is only known from five ancient manuscripts, all of which are dated fourteen hundred years after he penned his works.

The Bible is even more accurate than ancient historians. Dr. Robert Wilson has been called "the outstanding authority on ancient languages of the Middle East." While investigating the Bible's record of kings that ruled the area, he found only two or three misspellings in the Bible of the twenty-nine kings' names when compared to unearthed monuments that listed their names.

Compare that with a list of Egyptian kings uncovered at an archeological dig of a Greek library thought to have been used in 200 B.C. Of the thirty-eight Egyptian kings listed, only three or four of them could be verified by other archeological evidence. The famous second-century historian Ptolemy drew up a list of the eighteen kings of Babylon. Not one of them is spelled correctly when compared to ancient Babylonian monuments.

Wilson claims, "If anyone talks against the Bible, ask him about the kings mentioned in it. There are twenty-nine kings of Egypt, Israel, Moab, Damascus, Tyre, Babylon, Assyria, and Persia referred to and ten different countries among these twenty-nine; all of which are included in the Bible accounts and on ancient monuments. Every one of these is given his right name in the Bible, his right country, and placed in the correct chronological order."[8]

The Bible continues to stand up to historical and archeological testing. For another example, many secular historians have dismissed Luke's account. But Luke points out the historical accuracy of his Gospel with these words:

> Several biographies of Christ have already been written using as their source material the reports circulating among us from the early disciples and other eyewitnesses. However, it occurred to me that it would be well to recheck all these accounts from first to last and after thorough investigation to pass

this summary on to you, to reassure you of the truth of all you were taught. (Luke 1:1-4)

Luke, who was highly educated as a medical doctor, claims to have "rechecked all these accounts" and made a "thorough investigation." If the Bible is to be credible, it must stand up to historical investigation.

About this time Caesar Augustus, the Roman emperor, decreed that a census should be taken throughout the nation. (This census was taken when Quirinius was governor of Syria.)
    Everyone was required to return to his ancestral home for this registration. (Luke 2:1-3)

Skeptics claimed there was no census during that time, that Quirinius was not the governor of Syria and that no one had to return to his ancestors' home to register. If these charges are true, then the Bible's writers are hardly credible!

But archeologists have discovered that Caesar Augustus did indeed demand a census every fourteen years, one of which occurred around 9–8 B.C. (Because of a mistake in ancient calendars, Jesus was born seven years "before Christ.") Ancient writings found in Antioch do verify that Quirinius was governor of Syria around 7–6 B.C. And finally, an ancient inscription declares, "Because of the approaching census it is necessary that all those residing for any cause away from their homes should at once prepare to return to their own governments in order that they may complete the family registration of enrollment."[9]

Unlike Edgar Cayce's hypothetical history, the biblical accounts can be supported and proven by archeological discoveries. Cayce's "Atlantis" is yet to be discovered.

Does the Bible pass the four tests we proposed? It seems to be extremely accurate when recording history. And its prophecies relating to the birth, death, and resurrection of Christ appear to be unbelievably accurate. So, if this is true, it would appear that we can trust what the Bible says about the future as well. Believing that there is a heaven and hell—because an incredibly reliable source claims it exists—doesn't require too much more faith than believing that Julius Caesar ruled Rome.

201

"Hmmmm," Jana finally said after an hour of give-and-take. "You've given me a lot to think about."

"All I'm asking you to do is to consider the evidence for Christianity," I replied.

"But what if it really *is* wrong?" Jana continued. "You can't be 100 percent sure."

"You're right, we can't be 100 percent sure about anything. There's a slight—really slight—possibility that you and this camp are simply a figment of my imagination. The mosquitoes here seem awfully real, though. But let's say, just for the sake of argument," I continued, "that Christianity isn't the only way. I've still lived a life that's filled with love, joy, and peace following this 'false' Christ. These 'misguided' principles have caused me to live a healthy life and enjoy an incredible love life with my wife—and only my wife. So I don't have any concerns about STDs or Lois comparing me to other lovers. I wake up with the assurance—even if it's completely 'wrong'—that God is somehow going to work all that comes my way, good and bad, to the good. And if I die and there is no heaven or hell, I won't regret a thing. But," I cautioned, "what if I reject Christ and then discover he was telling the truth—that there really is a heaven and hell—and I'm going to the hotter location?"

"So you win either way. If you're right, you live in heaven, and if you're wrong, you've enjoyed this life."

"Yeah, that's right."

19

Is There Really a Heaven?

In the hit movie *My Girl,* Vada, the undertaker's ten-year-old daughter, tells her best friend, Thomas J., her idea of heaven:

> I think that everyone gets their own horse or their own bike or car or whatever it is they like to ride. And all they do is ride them and eat whatever they want all day long. And everybody is best friends with everybody else, and when they play sports, there are no teams so no one gets picked last. And you don't have to be scared of that. Actually, nobody's scared of anything. And nobody has allergies or gets sick. And they take care of each other, like friends. And . . . nobody has to die.[1]

Is there really a heaven with golden streets—for Vada and Thomas J. to ride bicycles?

As we mentioned in chapter 18, the Bible is an incredibly accurate book historically and prophetically. We can be very sure that what it says about the afterlife is equally accurate.

The "Soul" Survivor

Before we discuss the biblical account of the afterlife, we first have to discuss what part of us survives after life.

In the story of creation we read, "The Lord God

formed the man from the dust of the ground and breathed into his nostrils the breath of life, and the man became a living being [or soul]" (Genesis 2:7, NIV).

God created us with not only a physical body, but an eternal soul: that unique part of us that includes our personality and character—the real me that makes me *me* and the real you that makes you *you*. Throughout Scripture the inspired authors wrote of humans as having souls or spirits.[2]

Jesus taught the existence of the soul when he commanded his followers to "love the Lord your God with all your heart, and with all your soul, and with all your strength, and with all your mind" (Luke 10:27). He made it clearer that the body and soul are separate when he spoke of persecution: "Do not be afraid of those who kill the body but cannot kill the soul" (Matthew 10:28, NIV).

Why does God make us go through life on earth if he knows that heaven is much better?

The Bible's definition of death, then, is separation of the soul from the body. We see death explained this way throughout the Old Testament.[3]

We see the same concept in the New Testament when Jesus raised Jairus's daughter from the dead: "He took her by the hand and said, 'My child, get up!' Her spirit returned, and at once she stood up" (Luke 8:54-55, NIV).

While Jesus was on the cross, he "called out with a loud voice, 'Father, into your hands I commit my spirit.' When he had said this, he breathed his last" (Luke 23:41, NIV).

The Bible, then, clearly claims that each of us has an eternal soul or spirit that becomes separated from our earthly body at death.

Does this mean that, as one author claims, "death is a friend to be embraced"? From the creation of life in the book of Genesis to the destruction of death in the book of Revelation, the importance of physical, earthly life is stressed.

In the Gospels we find Jesus and his disciples healing the sick and even raising the dead. If our earthly life were merely something to be endured before we could enjoy heavenly life, then it would be absolutely cruel for Christ to heal the sick—and even more so to bring the dead back from heaven to some horrible "vale of tears."

How spiritual do you have to be to go to heaven?

Christians are sometimes accused of just biding their time until the sweet by-and-by. And yet Christ's ministry validated the importance of physical life. Throughout Scripture, death is viewed as "an enemy" (1 Corinthians 15:26).

The apostle Paul seems to imply that life here on earth is beneficial:

For to me, living means opportunities for Christ, and dying—well, that's better yet! But if living will give me more opportunities to win people to Christ, then I really don't know which is better, to live or die! Sometimes I want to live, and at other times I don't, for I long to go and be with Christ. How much happier for *me* than being here! But the fact is that I can be of more help to *you* by staying! (Philippians 1:21-24)

For instance, I have a friend who suffered severe heart failure. As a result of blood not getting to her brain, she's somewhat brain damaged. To make things even more tragic, she had a brilliant mind before her cardiac arrest. With the dazed expression of someone who is mentally impaired, she keeps asking, "Why didn't God just take me? Why did he leave me here like this?" I have no answer except to tell her, "God puts real value on life and living—regardless of our 'quality of life.'"

So we are commanded to take care of our physical as well as spiritual needs. The Bible never "glorifies" death.

Amazing Grace

In addition to the concept of the soul or spirit, we need to understand how souls are judged in the afterlife. Will Mother Teresa go to heaven because she gave unselfishly to help the poor? Will Adolph Hitler go to hell because he was responsible for the deaths of more than 10 million people? The Bible's answer is no:

> For it is by grace you have been saved, through faith—and this not from yourselves, it is the gift of God—not by works, so that no one can boast. (Ephesians 2:8-9, NIV)

> You see, at just the right time, when we were still powerless, Christ died for the ungodly. Very rarely will anyone die for a righteous man, though for a good man someone might possibly dare to die. But God demonstrates his own love for us in this: While we were still sinners, Christ died for us. Since we have now been justified by his blood, how much more shall we be saved from God's wrath through him! (Romans 5:6-9, NIV)

At what age can you go to heaven or hell?

Our fate for eternity is determined by acceptance or rejection of Jesus Christ as our Lord and Savior—not by our good or bad actions, or our degree of "spirituality." (We'll talk more about that in chapter 21.) So when we talk about the "believing dead" and the "unbelieving dead," it is not the "good" dead and the "bad" dead, but those who have believed Christ's claims and those who have rejected them.

Many believe that God's grace extends to those who are too young (babies, young children) or not mentally competent (the mentally retarded or mentally ill) to make a choice. If they can't make a deliberate choice between believing or rejecting Christ, then they go to heaven.

Sheol/Hades

On my survey, young people wanted to know: **Where do our souls go after death? . . . to a holding tank? . . . to wait in the grave? . . . to a waiting room? Isn't there a place between heaven and hell?**

Unfortunately, there is no chapter in the Bible entitled "Everything We Ever Wanted to Know about the Afterlife." We are left to piece together clues that are scattered throughout Scripture. So what follows, admittedly, is some amateur detective work. Other investigators may come up with slightly different interpretations, but I've tried to examine various Scriptures as carefully as my undergraduate degree in theology and my graduate work in journalism will allow.

Where do you go immediately after you die?

The Old Testament seems to teach that after death every soul goes to "Sheol, the place of the departed dead."[4] Unfortunately, the first two-thirds of the Bible says very little about the living conditions in Sheol. We're simply told that it is the place of the dead's souls.

In the New Testament, Christ sheds light on "Sheol" (which is called "Hades" in Greek) with his parable of the rich man and Lazarus (see chapter 16 for the story). According to this parable, Hades is divided into two camps separated by a "great gulf." On the one side are the believing dead who are "being comforted," and on the other side are the unbelieving dead who are in "torment" and "anguish" (Luke 16:19-31).

When Christ tells the repentant thief, who is also being crucified on a cross, "Today you will be with me in Paradise" (Luke 23:43), he is referring to the good side of the great gulf. .

Heaven

Many dramatic changes occurred after Christ died on the cross. The huge curtain in the Jewish temple, which separated the average person from the presence of God, was supernaturally ripped from top to bottom (Matthew 27:51). This symbolically announced that now, through Christ's death, every person—not just the high priest—had access to God. No longer would people have to bring sacrifices for the forgiveness of their sins. Christ had become the perfect sacrifice to make a way for all people who believed on him to have access to God (Hebrews 10:1-22). We'll talk more about that in chapter 21.

Can you see what's happening on earth from heaven?

The apostle Paul writes that while Christ was in the grave for three days he descended into "the lower earthly regions" (Hades) and brought the righteous dead out to be with him in heaven (Ephesians 4:9-10).

The believing dead now go to be with Christ in heaven according to Paul:

> Now we look forward with confidence to our heavenly bodies, realizing that every moment we spend in these earthly bodies is time spent away from our eternal home in heaven with Jesus. We know these things are true by believing, not by seeing.

And we are not afraid but are quite content to die, for then we will be at home with the Lord. (2 Corinthians 5:6-8)

While believers are "home with the Lord" they still apparently keep an eye on earth. After listing many Bible heroes of faith, the author of Hebrews speaks of them as a "great cloud of witnesses" (Hebrews 12:1). Many commentators believe this implies that those who have gone before us are cheering on earthly believers as they "run with perseverance the race marked out for [them]."

Resurrection Power

The story of the afterlife doesn't end with the believers with Christ in heaven and the unbelievers in Hades. The Bible also claims that all the dead bodies—which after centuries are nothing but dust—will be "resurrected," or brought back to life.

What will our heavenly bodies be like?

Daniel prophesies, "And many of those whose bodies lie dead and buried will rise up, some to everlasting life and some to shame and everlasting contempt" (12:2).

Jesus taught, "Don't be so surprised! Indeed the time is coming when all the dead in their graves shall hear the voice of God's Son, and shall rise again—those who have done good, to eternal life; and those who have continued in evil, to judgment" (John 5:28-29).

The apostle Paul writes:

The bodies we have now embarrass us, for they become sick and die; but they will be full of glory when we come back to life again. Yes, they are weak, dying bodies now, but when we live again they will be full of strength. They are just human bodies at death, but when they come back to life they will be superhuman bodies. (1 Corinthians 15:43-44)

210

According to various Scriptures there will be two separate resurrections of earthly bodies:

For the Lord himself will come down from heaven with a mighty shout and with the soul-stirring cry of the archangel and the great trumpet-call of God. And the believers who are dead will be the first to rise to meet the Lord. (1 Thessalonians 4:16)

This is the First Resurrection. . . . For them the Second Death holds no terrors, for they will be priests of God and of Christ, and shall reign with him a thousand years. (Revelation 20:5-6)

From these verses it appears that those who believe in Christ as their Savior will be reunited with their resurrected body and will reign with Christ during a thousand-year period of earthly peace. (The unbelieving dead apparently are still in torment on the wrong side of the gulf in Hades.)

Is there sex in heaven?

This "heavenly body" will be like Christ's resurrected body: It was apparently different in appearance so his closest friends didn't immediately recognize him. But they did recognize his voice and personality. Some have suggested that we will know others in heaven by their unique characteristics, rather than by their appearance (1 Corinthians 13:12). Christ's resurrected body wasn't a ghostly form—it could be touched and could eat a meal (Luke 24:38-43). In fact, Revelation reveals that we'll do a lot of eating in heaven. (Now that will be heaven—a seven-year feast, and we won't gain a pound!)

One part of heavenly bodies that didn't appeal to me, as a teen, was the unisex design: "Jesus replied, 'Marriage is for people here on earth, but when those who are counted worthy of being raised from the dead get to heaven, they do not marry'" (Luke 20:34-35). What, *no sex?* But Paul reveals that sex is a symbol of the incredible joy we will have in heaven (Ephesians 5:31-32). I deal with this in the chapter "Why Sexuality?" in *Sex Is Not a Four-Letter Word*. So earthly intercourse is just a sample of the pleasures of heaven. Wow!

Christ's new body also could walk though solid doors (John 20:19) and float through the sky (Acts 1:9).

Although that sounds incredible, some explain it as simply having a multidimensional body. Our lives now are bound by a three-dimensional prison of height, width, and depth.

To help understand this, imagine we lived in a two-dimensional world of only height and width. We would be bound to our flat world just as these ink spots are bound to this flat page. If someone arrived from a three-dimensional universe—a place that knew depth—he would seem to have remarkable powers. By simply moving from this page to the next he would seem to have disappeared, because all we know is this two-dimensional page that we are confined to.

Are there real mansions in heaven?

Perhaps our heavenly bodies will be multidimensional—able to do things that are impossible in a three-dimensional universe. And if that isn't mind-boggling enough, perhaps heaven and hell are not far off, but right here with us—simply in a different dimension.

These new bodies may be the "mansions" that Jesus promises: "There are many homes up there where my Father lives, and I am going to prepare them for your coming. When everything is ready, then I will come and get you, so that you can always be with me where I am" (John 14:2-3).

Paul speaks of these "homes" as new bodies:

> For we know that when this tent we live in now is taken down—when we die and leave these bodies—we will have wonderful new bodies in heaven, homes that will be ours forevermore, made for us by God himself and not by human hands. How weary we grow of our present bodies. That is why we look forward eagerly to the day when we shall have heavenly bodies that we shall put on like new clothes. For we shall not be merely spirits without bodies. (2 Corinthians 5:1-3)

At the end of the thousand-year reign of Christ, there will be a final battle between the forces of God and evil (Armageddon), and then Satan will be thrown into the lake of fire along with all those who didn't choose to believe in Christ for their salvation. (We'll talk more about this in the next chapter.)

Is heaven really a literal place with gold streets and all?

Several teens asked, **"How can I enjoy heaven if I know that some of my friends and family are in hell?"** Job—who had a lot of questions—may have the answer: "Death consumes sinners as drought and heat consume snow. Even the sinner's own mother shall forget him. . . . No one will remember him any more" (Job 24:19-20). It seems that God will completely erase any memory of our friends and family who aren't in heaven with us.

What we *will* be conscious of is revealed in the book of Revelation:

Then I saw a new earth (with no oceans!) and a new sky, for the present earth and sky had disappeared. And I, John, saw the Holy City, the new Jerusalem, coming down from God out of heaven. . . .

In a vision [the angel] took me to a towering mountain peak, and from there I watched that wondrous city, the holy Jerusalem, descending out of the skies from God. It was filled with the glory of God and flashed and glowed like a precious gem, crystal clear like jasper. Its walls were broad and high, with twelve gates guarded by twelve angels. And the

What is heaven like? names of the twelve tribes of Israel were written on the gates. There were three gates on each side—north, south, east, and west. The walls had twelve foundation stones, and on them were written the names of the twelve apostles of the Lamb.

The angel held in his hand a golden measuring stick to measure the city and its gates and walls. When he measured it, he found it was a square as wide as it was long; in fact it was in the form of a cube, for its height was exactly the same as its other dimensions—1,500 miles each way. Then he measured the thickness of the walls and found them to be 216 feet across (the angel called out these measurements to me, using standard units).

The city itself was pure, transparent gold like glass! The wall was made of jasper, and was built on twelve layers of foundation stones inlaid with gems: The first layer with jasper; the second with sapphire; the third with chalcedony; the fourth with emerald; the fifth with sardonyx; the sixth layer with sardus; the seventh with chrysolite; the eighth with beryl; the ninth with topaz; the tenth with chrysoprase; the eleventh with jacinth; the twelfth with amethyst.

The twelve gates were made of pearls—each gate from a single pearl! And the main street was pure, transparent gold, like glass.

No temple could be seen in the city, for the Lord God Almighty and the Lamb are worshiped in it everywhere. And the city has no need of sun or moon to light it, for the glory of God and of the Lamb illuminate it. Its light will light the nations of the earth, and the rulers of the world will come and bring their glory to it. Its gates never close; they stay open all day long—and there is no night! And the glory and honor of all the nations shall be brought into it. Nothing evil will be permitted in it—no one immoral or dishonest—but only those whose names are written in the Lamb's Book of Life.

And he pointed out to me a river of pure Water of Life, clear as crystal, flowing from the throne of God and the Lamb, coursing down the center of the main street. On each side of the river grew Trees of Life, bearing twelve crops of fruit, with a fresh crop each month; the leaves were used for medicine to heal the nations.

Are there animals and pets in heaven?

There shall be nothing in the city that is evil; for the throne of God and of the Lamb will be there, and his servants will worship him. And they shall see his face; and his name shall be written on their foreheads. And there will be no night there—no need for lamps or sun—for the Lord God will be their light; and they shall reign forever and ever. (Revelation 21:1-2, 10–22:5)

While no animals are mentioned in this account, the prophet Isaiah writes:

In that day the wolf and the lamb will lie down together, and the leopard and goats will be at peace. Calves and fat cattle will be safe among lions, and a little child shall lead them all. The cows will graze among bears; cubs and calves will lie down together. . . . Babies will crawl safely among poisonous snakes, and a little child who puts his hand in a nest of deadly adders will pull it out unharmed. Nothing will hurt or destroy in all my holy mountain, for as the waters fill the sea, so shall the earth be full of the knowledge of the Lord. (Isaiah 11:6-9)

Are you the same age in heaven as you were when you died?

If this prophetic passage is a literal description of heaven, it would appear that there will be animals, that all will be vegetarians (what, no Big Macs?), and that human heavenly bodies will be in the form of babies, little children, and adults.

And that brings us to another question about heaven. Are there literally gates of pearl, golden streets, and friendly lions? Let me say with absolute certainty—I have no idea! It's possible that the prophets used word pictures because they couldn't put the incredible beauty of heaven into human terms. The best they could do is write, "This place is so fantastic that they use giant pearls for city gates and pave streets with gold. The peace will be so strong that meat-eating lions will become best friends with their former diet of mutton."

If it is literal, it will be incredible. If it's not literal, it will be beyond incredible!

20
Is There Really a Hell?

A Texas newspaper reports:

> Rev. Bill Lane who . . . preaches "hellfire, damna-
> tion, and brimstone" added something new to his
> "preachin'." Suddenly the not-so-hot evangelist
> became one of the hottest evangelists in the country.
> Literally. He set himself on fire while giving a sermon
> on hell. The idea caught on like wildfire and soon [he]
> was known to millions as the Flaming Evangelist.
>
> Already, Rev. Lane has set himself on fire 75
> times and has only been burned badly once. [He]
> wears a specially treated undershirt and shirt to pre-
> vent the fire from burning through.
>
> While the flames are raging, Bill points to the
> crowd with a flaming finger and shouts, "You may
> not like what you are seeing, but imagine this for
> eternity." [1]

Is there really a hell? Let's take a look at some ideas.

Not Quite Hell
The Roman Catholic church teaches that purgatory is an
intermediate state between heaven and hell.

218

Purgatory: A place of temporal punishment for those who die in God's grace, but are not entirely free from venial [less serious] sins or have not entirely paid the satisfaction due to their sins. The existence of purgatory is universally taught by all the Fathers of the Church. The words of our Lord, "Thou shalt not come out from it until thou hast paid the last penny" are very clear (Matthew 5:25-26). Later, when speaking of the sins against the Holy Ghost, Jesus says that such a sin "will not be forgiven either in this world or in the next," thus implying that there are some sins that can be atoned for in the next world (Matthew 12:32).

Is there some place between heaven and hell?

Saint Paul also shows his belief in purgatory when, in his second letter to Timothy, he prays for the deceased Onesiphorus. "May the Lord grant him to find mercy from the Lord on that day" (2 Timothy 1:18). Even in the Old Testament there was a belief in the existence of purgatory, for there we find Judas Maccabeus sending 12,000 drachmas to Jerusalem to have sacrifices offered for the sins of the dead. That chapter ends with the advice: "It is therefore a holy and wholesome thought to pray for the dead, that they may be loosed from sins" (2 Maccabees 12:46).

In purgatory, souls suffer for a while in satisfaction for their sins before they can enter heaven. The principal suffering of these souls consists in the pain of experiencing, on one hand, an intense longing for God and, on the other, a realization that they are hindered from possessing Him by reason of their past sins. Unlike the souls in hell, they are certain of one day seeing God. They can be helped, moreover, by the prayers of the faithful on earth, and especially by offering of Mass.[2]

Protestants would protest (thus the name Protestant) the doctrine on several points. First, the word *purgatory* is not found in either the Protestant or Catholic Bible.

Second, the foundation of the Protestant Reformation was the concept of salvation by grace—not human works. The Catholic Bible itself teaches "for by grace you have been saved through faith; and that not of yourselves, for it is a gift of God; not as the outcome of works, lest anyone may boast" (Ephesians 2:8-9, *The Catholic Bible*). And there is no need for additional purification, as the Catholic Bible states: "If we acknowledge our sins, [Christ] is faithful and just to forgive us our sins and cleanse us from *all* iniquity" (1 John 1:9, *The Catholic Bible,* italics mine).

219

Are you

really

judged?

Protestants also have problems with the arguments presented in favor of purgatory. This doctrine was not taught until the seventh century, so early church fathers did not subscribe to such a teaching. In Matthew 5 Jesus is actually talking about earthly court systems. And Onesiphorus was not dead yet when Paul wrote 2 Timothy. Protestants also question the reliability of the book of Maccabees, since neither Jesus nor any of his disciples ever quoted from it or made reference to it. Thus, it is not included in the Protestant Bible.

Finally, it would seem that the thief crucified with Jesus would need to spend some time in purgatory for his many sins. And yet Jesus promises the repentant criminal, "Today you will be with me in Paradise. This is a solemn promise" (Luke 23:43).

While there isn't anything specifically about purgatory in Scripture, there are some very detailed descriptions of hell.

Hell

As we discussed earlier, the bodies of the unbelieving dead are left on the bad side of the gulf in Hades until the final Judgment Day.

220

And I saw a great white throne and the one who sat upon it, from whose face the earth and sky fled away, but they found no place to hide. I saw the dead, great and small, standing before God; and The Books were opened, including the Book of Life. And the dead were judged according to the things written in The Books, each according to the deeds he had done. The oceans surren-dered the bodies buried in them; and the earth and the underworld gave up the dead in them. Each was judged according to his deeds. And Death and Hell were thrown into the Lake of Fire. This is the Second Death—the Lake of Fire. And if anyone's name was not found recorded in the Book of Life, he was thrown into the Lake of Fire. (Revelation 20:11-15)

Is there really fire in hell?

But is this a real, literal "lake of fire"? Again, let me say with absolute certainty—I have no idea!

Jesus spoke of hell throughout the Gospels. The Greek word he uses is *Gehenna,* which comes from the Hebrew word *Ghi-Hinnom,* or Valley of Hinnom. Located just west and southwest of Jerusalem, there was a literal Gehenna. Here, parents had forced their children to walk through fire fueled by brimstone in worship to the false god Molech (2 Kings 23:10; Isaiah 30:33). During Christ's time, Gehenna was a constantly burning landfill. Often garbage would lodge in the rocks above it and breed maggots. This may explain the description of the fire of *gehenna,* "where the worm never dies, and the fire never goes out—where all are salted with fire" (Mark 9:47-49).

Throughout Scripture fire is used as a symbol for something greater or more fearful. So if "hellfire and brimstone" are figurative, this means that hell is something far worse than literal burning.

Separation from God seems to be taught as the "hell-ish" part of hell:

> The Lord Jesus [will appear] suddenly from heaven in flaming fire with his mighty angels, bringing judgment on those who do not wish to know God and who refuse to accept his plan to save them through our Lord Jesus Christ. They will be punished in everlasting hell, forever separated from the Lord, never to see the glory of his power. (2 Thessalonians 1:7-9)

Seven times the Gospels speak of hell as "outer darkness . . . the place of weeping and torment" (Matthew 8:12; 13:42, 50; 22:13; 24:51; 25:30; and Luke 13:28).

Do you get a choice between heaven and hell?

Jesus warns us that the "cursed ones"—those who have refused to accept his offer of salvation—"shall go away into eternal punishment; but the righteous into everlasting life" (Matthew 25:46). In other words, the punishment of unbelievers will be the exact same length as the reward of the believers—eternity (Daniel 12:2; Matthew 18:8; Mark 3:29; 9:44-48; Jude 13).

But the good news is that God "is not willing that any should perish" (2 Peter 3:9). "For God loved the world so much that he gave his only Son so that anyone who believes in him shall not perish but have eternal life. God did not send his Son into the world to condemn it, but to save it" (John 3:16-17).

We send *ourselves* to hell by rejecting his gracious offer of eternal life. (We'll talk about how we accept this offer in the next chapter.)

21
I Don't Have a Question

In response to my survey concerning "a question(s) I have about the possibility of life after death," a fifteen-year-old wrote:

> **I don't have a question, but I have a question for you. I believe that the afterlife is not just a possibility, but that there is life in either heaven or hell. Jesus Christ is my Savior and Lord and I know where I am going. Do you?**

I have to admit that while in junior high I wasn't sure where I was going. For instance, one day I came home to an empty, silent house. The lights were on. But no sign of life. Then it hit me like a ton of Bibles. It could only mean one thing: Christ had returned "like a thief in the night" and snatched up Mom, Dad, my brother, and Buster (our Boston bull terrier).

For years I had lived under apocalyptic terror that I would be living a "good Christian life," but in a moment of weakness, I would sin. And then—at that very instant, even before I could ask forgiveness—Christ would return for his faithful followers.

Now I was left behind, all alone to face the battle of Armageddon and then the fires of hell!

Suddenly, my conscience recalled the reason for my doom. Just an hour before, my little brother had ridden my new bike into the side of the garage. And in the emotion of the moment, I had called him a name. Not just any name, but the four-letter name that my pastor warned would guarantee a ticket straight down—or at least keep one from going straight up at Christ's return.

Yes, I had called my brother a F-O-O-L! And according to my pastor's interpretation of Matthew 5:22, there was nothing left to do but flick on the TV and wait for Emergency Broadcast System announcements.

But then to my rapturous relief, my family and Buster returned from visiting the neighbors. While comforted that I had one more chance, my fear that one sin would disqualify me from heaven continued to haunt me.

It wasn't until my college Greek class that I discovered that not every sin sends us to hell.

In the broadest definition, sin is any action or attitude that is not motivated by love for God, for others, or for ourselves. Christ makes this clear when he declares that the most important commandments are to "love the Lord your God with all your heart and with all your soul and with all your mind . . . [and to] love your neighbor as yourself" (Matthew 22:37-39, NIV).

So I did sin by not having loving attitudes toward my brother. But under this broad definition of sin, there are different types of sins.

For instance, the apostle Paul writes that "all have *sinned*" (Romans 3:23, NIV).

We would say that a minister who uses pastoral influence to lure others into sexual activity has *sinned*.

A drug-dealing pimp with a criminal record as long as his stretch limo has *sinned*.

A person who chooses to reject God has *sinned*.

And a person whom God tells to "depart into utter darkness," has *sinned*.

While I've used the same English word in these five cases, the New Testament's original language distinguishes between them with five separate words—with five separate meanings.

225

Hamartia

Paul uses this Greek word in the sentence "for all have *hamartia*-ed and fall short of the glory of God." *Hamartia* describes actions and attitudes that "fall short" of God's perfection. I *hamartia*-ed when I yelled at my brother. We *hamartia* when we're impatient with the clerk at Burger King. We *hamartia* whenever our actions and attitudes are not completely Christlike.

Luke uses *hamartia* in his version of the Lord's Prayer: "Forgive us our *hamartia*s, for we also forgive everyone who *hamartia*s against us" (Luke 11:4, NIV). Christ implies that his followers do *hamartia*—fairly regularly!

John is even more direct. "If we claim to be without *hamartia*, we deceive ourselves and the truth is not in us" (1 John 1:8, NIV). But John encourages us by revealing that "there is *hamartia* that does not lead to death" (1 John 5:16, NIV).

Will just one sin send a person to hell?

Occasional *hamartia*, then, doesn't cancel one's reservations for heaven. But it musn't be ignored!

1. Admitting that we have "sinned" is the first step, then, to becoming a Christian. This sin has separated each of us from the loving (and sinless) God.

Kevin had attended church since he was old enough for the nursery. He was proud of his perfect attendance awards and of his avoidance of his Christian school's "sins."

But when he arrived at the public junior high, Kevin was

faced with everything his parents and the church had warned him against: drugs, cheating, obscenity, promiscuous sex, etc., etc. He found himself looking down on the other teens with a holier-than-thou attitude.

Most of all, he saw his real self. He realized that, although he was keeping the Ten Commandments, he wasn't doing very well with the command to love his neighbors.

Even people like Kevin, who live "good" lives, have to admit that they have broken God's commandments to fully love God and their neighbor as themselves.

2. The second step is to believe (based on the reliable evidence in chapter 18) that Jesus Christ—God-in-flesh—came to earth to take the punishment for our unloving (sinful) actions and attitudes.

When we were utterly helpless, with no way of escape, Christ came at just the right time and died for us sinners who had no use for him. . . . But God showed his great love for us by sending Christ to die for us while we were still sinners. And since by his blood he did all this for us as sinners, how much more will he do for us now that he has declared us not guilty? Now he will save us from all of God's wrath to come. And since, when we were his enemies, we were brought back to God by the death of his Son, what blessings he must have for us now that we are his friends and he is living within us! (Romans 5:6, 8-10)

Will God forgive me?

3. Finally, we must desire to express his love in every area of our life. Paul prays for the new Christians in Ephesus:

And I pray that Christ will be more and more at home in your hearts, living within you as you trust in him. May your roots go down deep into the soil of God's marvelous love; and may you be able to feel and understand, as all God's children should, how long, how wide, how deep, and how high his love really is; and to experience this love for yourselves, though it is so great that you will never . . . understand it. And so at last you will be filled up with God himself. (Ephesians 3:17-19)

But Christians will never love as perfectly as God loves, so believers must confess their unloving acts (*hamartia*s).

Adikia

While often translated "sin," *adikia* more accurately describes an action that is "a perversion of righteousness." The person who *adikia*s has lost sensitivity to God and views immoral actions as completely normal, even righteous.

The minister who uses parishioners sexually—and even believes this is spiritually helpful for them—is sinning in this manner. The whole being is twisted toward impure living.

I was concerned about pleasing God in my actions and attitudes, so I wasn't *adikia*ing when I gave in to the temptation to tell my brother what I thought of him. And so I was still in relationship with God—and that is what determines where we spend eternity! The person who *adikia*s has willfully and deliberately turned away from God and his love and will spend eternity separated from God unless he or she restores that relationship with God through the three steps mentioned earlier.

Anomia

The drug-dealing pimp with twenty years in the business is living a life-style of sin. This is not the occasional whoops-I'm-sorry-God-I-won't-let-it-happen-again sin, but *anomia*. The apostle John speaks of this kind of continual sin: "No one who lives in [Christ] keeps on sinning. No one who continues to sin has either seen him or known him" (1 John 3:6, NIV).

Just as fish understand no other life than swimming, *anomia*-ers understand no other life than sinning. So while I *hamartia*-ed by calling my brother a "fool," I was still trying to live, as best I knew, a life that was pleasing to God and others. Therefore, I had not *anomia*-ed or disqualified myself from heaven.

Asebia

Asebia deals specifically with rebellion toward or rejection of God. The Lord will never cut off the believer who wants to please him and maintain a relationship with him.

Paul reminds us:

For I am convinced that nothing can ever separate us from his love. Death can't, and life can't. The angels won't, and all the powers of hell itself cannot keep God's love away. Our fears for today, our worries about tomorrow, or where we are—high above the sky, or in the deepest ocean—nothing will ever be able to separate us from the love of God demonstrated by our Lord Jesus Christ when he died for us. (Romans 8:38-39)

Does God decide who goes to heaven or hell? Can we choose heaven or hell?

However, we can choose to reject God—through active rebellion or passive indifference—and thus separate ourselves from him. The apostle Paul uses the word *asebia* when he describes the immorality and idolatry in the first chapter of Romans (verses 18-32).

My anger toward my brother was in no way a willful, conscious rejection of God, the Bible, or the church. I may have wanted to reject my brother, but I had not *asebia*-ed.

Parabasis

Finally, *parabasis* is a legal term for "guilt and condemnation." This term was reserved for condemned criminals: "Guilty as charged!" But Christians don't live under God's gavel of judgment:

> There is now awaiting no condemnation for those who belong to Christ Jesus. (Romans 8:1)

> [God's] love is made complete among us so that we will have confidence on the day of judgment. (1 John 4:17, NIV)

For believers who have sincerely asked forgiveness for past sins (all varieties) and desire to daily love God, others, and themselves, there is no *parabasis.*

There will be times when Christians will sin—*hamartia*—by falling short of God's perfection. And this shouldn't be taken lightly, but confessed. I not only had to ask God for forgiveness, but I had to ask my little brother as well.

These occasional *hamartia*s, however, do not earn one an overheated eternity—unless the believer chooses to reject God (*asebia*), live a life-style of immorality (*anomia*) and unrighteousness (*adikia*), and refuse God's forgiveness (*parabasis*).

Do you go to heaven or hell because of what you've done?

But I do wish my parents had told me they were going over to the neighbors! Or better yet, that someone had told me that one *hamartia* by a believer won't send him or her to hell. Again, it is not our actions that determine our address in eternity—it is trusting in or rejecting Christ that does.

If you would like to know God in a personal way—and enjoy his love throughout eternity—you can read more about it in the book of 1 John, one of the last books in the Bible. Or you can ask a youth pastor or minister about it. Or write to me in care of Tyndale House Publishers (P.O. Box 80, Wheaton, IL 60189), and I'll send you some helpful material.

PART SIX

Why? Why? Why?

*I*t's possible that the same knife that killed Miss Yamagishi cut these slits in the picture," Sergeant Ryan observed matter-of-factly. "Both are daggers—knives with both edges sharp—and they seem to be identical in width." He carefully slipped the paper into a small plastic evidence bag. "And you're sure that this Stone knows that you think he killed the girl."

"He probably does. I guess I did tell a lot of people," Kathy replied sheepishly.

"Kathy, Kathy, Kathy." Mr. Norman sighed. "I asked you to keep a lid on this killing."

"Sorry," she mumbled.

Sergeant Ryan scanned the staff. "None of the rest of you told anyone what the two witnesses saw, did you? Think hard—did you tell anyone?"

Kevin, Lori, and Nate admitted telling their parents, but no one else.

"And you told them that this was highly confidential information?" Sgt. Ryan asked. All three nodded yes.

"So where do we go from here, Sergeant?" Mr. Norman asked.

Kathy interrupted. "You're not going to use me as bait to lure this sicko into a sting operation, are you?"

"No, miss. This isn't a TV cop show. We'll drive you home before we go to talk with Stone."

"But shouldn't I have twenty-four-hour protection?"

Ryan shook his head and turned to Mr. Norman. "Thanks for keeping this out of the school newspaper until we at least have a good suspect in custody. Then I'll give you some exclusive quotes that'll make the TV news people really envious. Until then, give me a call the second anything else suspicious happens. I don't know what kind of nut case we're dealing with."

With that, Sergeant Ryan escorted Kathy out of the office.

"Man," Kevin muttered. "We're sitting on the biggest story in Lakeshore history, and we can't print it."

"Not yet," Mr. Norman answered. "But when we do run it, we'll be able to go in-depth better than anyone else. Let's start with getting student reactions. Kevin and Lori, you two did a great job with the Brian McCarthy funeral; I'd like you two to cover Renee Roberts's today. Since we gave her front-page coverage Friday, let's run that inside— maybe with an editorial complimenting Mr. Coldwater for the way he handled the Traci Yamagishi killing. Nate, I want you to cover that killing. Write it two ways—one way if we can't print it as a murder and another way if Ryan takes the gag order off. We'll work together on it."

Kevin was hearing Mr. Norman's voice, but the words just weren't registering. Apparently the teacher sensed that.

"Maybe we just need to talk about what's happened the past couple weeks," the teacher suggested as he propped his feet up on his desk.

"Well," Lori began, "I think it's been hard to know how to react to all that's happened. I mean, I lost one of my grandmothers, but that's the only death I've experienced—until now. And she had been in a nursing home for years, so I guess it was expected. But I never expected any of my friends to die."

235

"Yeah. Why seems to be the big question, like I wrote in last week's column," Nate added. "And I guess I wonder how many more obituaries the Sentinel is going to run this year."

Kevin nodded in agreement. "And like Lori said, I think the school is really struggling to know how to grieve. I thought that Dr. Cooper was really helpful." He paused, then continued, "I guess grief is kinda like love. It's one of those emotions that nobody can tell you about until you personally experience it. And then it's really confusing because it's something so new and different from any other emotion."

"Well put, Kevin," Mr. Norman agreed. "There may be an editorial there. Why don't you work on it?"

"I guess," Kevin answered, then continued. "I think Mr. Coldwater is catching on that while it's true that life goes on, it goes on really differently after a death."

"Oh, that reminds me," Mr. Norman said, sitting up in his chair. "Mr. Coldwater gave me this news release from the Center on Disease Control with statistics on teenage AIDS cases and some practical reasons to 'just say no' to premarital sex. We're going to see a lot more obituaries in high-school papers if these projections are correct. But anyway, he said—are you ready for this?—maybe we should run an article about it!"

Friday, the Lakeshore Sentinel carried the banner headline, "Lakeshore Student Arrested in Brutal Death of Classmate."

Jonathan "Jake" Stone, an eighteen-year-old junior, was arrested Monday along with two other adults in the stabbing death of Traci Yamagishi, 15, a sophomore, last Thursday.

Yamagishi's nude body was found in a vacant lot between the school and the Lakeshore Estates housing development. Police report her neck was cut and her chest was cut in a cross-shaped pattern. There was no evidence of sexual abuse.

In an exclusive interview with Lakeshore Police, Sgt. Russ Ryan said that a tip by Sentinel assistant editor Kathy Rodriguez led police to suspect Stone in the killing.

Rodriguez became suspicious due to Stone's apparent fascination with the occult and satanism, which was verified by his computer record of borrowing library and video materials on the subject. When Stone learned of Rodriguez's suspicions, he allegedly sent her a staff photograph with the same cross pattern cut into the picture.

Stone has admitted to sending the photo, but denies that he was involved in the actual killing of Yamagishi. The two adults, John Bristol, 19, and David Mellville, 21, also entered innocent pleas at their arraignments. All three are being held without bond.

Traci Yamagishi's funeral was held Wednesday (see "Students Say Good-bye" on page 2).

"Good issue, team." Mr. Norman congratulated the staff as he admired the latest edition. "Mr. Coldwater was even complimentary. I think we have a good chance to win some *awards at the Quill and Scroll competition this year. Each of you has done a great job with—" Mr. Norman suddenly stopped mid-sentence and his eyes began to water. "You've done a great job with some of the toughest assignments you'll ever face." The teacher made eye contact with each editor as he slowly continued. "You've shown that you all have tough hides and tender hearts. I'm proud of each of you."*

Mr. Norman wiped his eyes and then flicked off the office light. "Have a good weekend," he said as he left the office.

"Ah, Lori . . ." Kevin felt his heart beat nervously as they found themselves walking alone in the hallway. "Ah, do you have plans for the weekend?"

"No. What do you have in mind?" Lori asked.

"Well, I was wondering if you'd like to go to a movie."

"You mean a date?"

Kevin felt his chest tighten and his mouth go dry as Lori's question pin-balled through the empty hallways. "Well, yeah," he answered.

"I'd like that, as long as the movie isn't Varsity Death Squad."

Kevin began to relax. "No way, but I've heard good reviews of More Than Friends—*if you're interested."*

"Yeah, I like the sound of that," Lori answered, and she moved closer as they walked. So do I, *Kevin thought as he caught their reflection in the school's trophy case.*

22
I Still Have a Question

Computer printers make me nervous. My stomach feels as if it, too, is being dragged through the tractor feed and into the roller. My heart keeps rhythm with the five-hundred-words-per-minute print head. My eyes track the newly formed letters as my thoughts of the moment are permanently pounded onto paper.

What I have written in the past ten months will be edited, typeset, printed, bound, and shipped off to bookstores as the authoritative answer to questions about death.

Maybe that's why *my* head is pounding along with the print head!

I've tried to verify and document each answer through personal interviews and hundreds of hours of researching printed material. I think "Mr. Norman" would be proud of the research and writing. (I finally had to explain to the city librarian that I wasn't a potential mass murderer or necrophiliac, but was writing a book about death. I'm not sure she was convinced as I toted armloads of "death books" out the door every two weeks.)

But still, I feel like I've only scratched the surface of this deep, deep subject.

And while I've tried to honestly answer the hundreds of different questions on a thousand surveys, I'm still honestly baffled about death. (I'm certainly not like the fifteen-year-old who wrote on the survey, "I have no questions. I know everything.")

Therefore, *Death & Beyond* will probably answer a few of your questions and generate a lot more. I hope and pray I've given you enough leads that you can conduct your own investigation into this mysterious subject. The Notes section refers to many books that you may find helpful.

And so none of our thoughts are "final copy." God is always stretching us spiritually and mentally so that our attitudes, values, priorities, perspectives, knowledge, and relationships are constantly being revised and updated to conform more to Jesus, "the author and perfecter of our faith" (Hebrews 12:2, NIV).

With that in mind, why don't you and I just consider this book a rough draft? OK? Thanks!

I pray that you may enjoy good health and that all may go well with you, even as your soul is getting along well. (3 John 2, NIV)

Jim

Appendix A

A Special Message to Parents

Not another phone call," I sighed. During the first hour of work the phone had rung at least fifteen times. While serving as editorial director at a small publishing house, I was expected to know "Where's the copy for page three?" "Do you still have the press proofs for the cover of *Perfect Love?*" "Is *life-style* one word, two words, or is it hyphenated?"

I braced myself for another call from the press when my wife cried out over the phone line, "Dad's dead!"

"What?!"

"Mom called and said that Dad died this morning. He's dead!"

"OK, I'll be home as soon as I can tell my editor and fill her in on what needs to be done."

During the next hour I made fifteen calls to notify my boss, my editor, my editorial assistant, my parents, our pastor, and others who needed to know immediately.

The hardest task was helping then three-year-old Paul and eight-year-old Faith deal with the death of their grandfather.

Psychologist Maria Nagy has discovered from her research that children under five don't believe death is final. That's why Paul kept asking, "Why is Mom so *humongous* sad?" Between ages five and nine, youngsters begin to accept the finality of death but don't understand that they themselves must eventually die. Older children and teens begin to realize that they themselves are mortal.

How can we help our children and young people deal with the harsh reality of death?

Preparing

In the cases of cancer or AIDS, parents have time to prepare children for the death of a loved one. But in the event of an auto accident or stroke, death comes suddenly with no warning. Our children need to be prepared for death.

The responsibility rests on us parents. Some schools offer "death education" classes, but most of our young people's learning—unfortunately—comes from the media as we discussed in chapter 2.

We can use the media, however, to open discussion on the topic. The evening news provides many opportunities to bring up the subject with our kids: local auto accidents, murders, and suicides; deaths of famous people; international war casualties—the list is endless.

Hopefully, this book will be read by both young people and parents and help them to work through, together, the many questions that surround this still-taboo subject.

Telling

Announcing the death of a loved one to our child or teen is probably one of the hardest jobs of parenting. Often we ourselves are feeling intense emotion. It's difficult to tell our children that one of their grandparents—and one of our parents—has died.

Medical as well as mental health professionals agree that we should ease into the announcement. Here's a typical "script."

Often it begins with nonverbal communication: Our sad expression or tears.

"I'm afraid I have some very sad news." We're beginning to prepare our children for the bad news. We're also giving them freedom to feel sad concerning the news.

"Remember how the doctors were really worried about Grandpa's high blood pressure?" We've planted the thought that something very serious has happened to Grandpa. Notice how each phrase brings worse news.

"Grandpa had a very bad stroke, and the doctors did everything they could. [Pause]I'm afraid that Grandpa died."

Easing into the announcement does not mean being dishonest. Not being straightforward, even with small children, can be dangerous.

In chapter 10 we discussed the importance of using "the D-word" (*death*). If we tell a small child that a grandfather has "gone to sleep," the child may become afraid to go to bed, or the child will expect him to wake up soon. If we say, "God took him," the child may become angry at God for being so cruel (see chapter 4). Never teach a child something he or she will have to unlearn later in life.

Listening

Elizabeth Richter, author of *Losing Someone You Love,* interviewed teens who had lost a brother or sister to death. She writes, "The most obvious need expressed by all the young people I spoke with was a desperate desire to be heard and for their feelings to be accepted—not judged, not ignored. Their questions did not always require answers, but they longed for compassion and understanding." [1]

One of the hardest temptations for me, as a parent, is to try to "fix" the situation. As I mentioned in chapter 10, teens—and adults—need our ears more than our mouth.

Allow them to express themselves without our answers and clichés. When they ask a direct question, then a direct answer is appropriate—but allow them to ask.

Grieving

In the past, people were told not to cry out loud at funerals. Mourners were urged to dry their eyes, be brave, be strong, and not express grief. Tranquilizers kept emotions under control. Today, however, medical and psychological studies have revealed the importance of "good grief."

Children and teens look to adults for clues about how to grieve. That's why it's important that we are open with our own feelings and questions. Encourage your child or teen to cry when he feels like crying, to be silent when she doesn't want to talk. Allow them to work through, in their own way, the stages of mourning described in chapter 11.

Amy Hillyard Jensen, whose nine-year-old drowned and twenty-three-year-old was killed in an auto accident, suggests that people "deliberately take time to grieve. Review mementos. Play nostalgic music. Look at pictures and read old letters. One therapist often recommends one hour a day—a grieving prescription."[2]

During the mourning process, we need to make sure our young people are eating well and getting regular exercise. Often those in mourning lose their appetite and become inactive. A good diet and exercise actually speed up the recovery process through biochemical changes that reduce depression.

We do need to be watchful of destructive or "pathological grief" described in the next appendix. If these symptoms persist, then we need to get our children to professional help: a pastor, school counselor, youth worker, or mental health professional.

Being There

As I mentioned in chapter 10, often just being there—without answers and clichés—is the best support.

Funeral director Jim Stone urges parents to go to the funeral home with their teen who has lost a friend or classmate. "Your young person needs your support during this very difficult time," he stresses.

It's always important to spend time with our children and young people, but it's absolutely essential to spend special time with them following a death. Take your child out to eat—just Dad and son, or Mom and daughter. Work on projects together. Do whatever brings the two of you together for an hour or two of uninterrupted time.

We need to keep in mind that the mourning process can often take one or more *years* to work through. Most of all, assure your young person that grief is a very normal emotion and is shared by every other person who has lost a loved one.

Appendix B

A Special Message to Teachers and Youth Leaders

More and more teens die each year from alcohol-related accidents, drive-by shootings, suicide, and AIDS.

As teachers and youth leaders, we will be called upon more and more to provide answers and support to our young people as they confront the realities of death and dying.

As mentioned in chapter 11, grief is the emotion of loss; mourning is the lengthy process of dealing with grief. And grief is a normal, natural part of losing someone we love. I believe our task, then, is to help our students or teen group understand the normal, natural stages of grief.

Marge Cavanaugh is a counselor at West Noble High School. In February three students were killed in an automobile accident. "The deaths hurt all of us—staff and students. But some positive things came out of it," she noted as we talked about the deaths.

Marge and her staff were prepared for such a tragedy by a crisis plan that had been formulated by the school corporation two years before the school's first death.

1. Building principal is designated to form a crisis management team in each school to deal with crisis.

2. Superintendent or designee will be in charge of media and outside operations (ministers, counseling agencies).

3. Inform staff exactly what happened. Get facts.

4. Staff meeting with students. Teachers are asked to review known facts and dispel rumors. Give only information needed. Staff are encouraged to allow for the expression of grief in their classes in whatever way is appropriate for students. (*All* responses are acceptable, from severe reactions to no reactions at all. Be aware of students who are at risk during classroom discussion.) The guiding principle is to return to normal routine within each class as soon as possible. Whenever and wherever possible, teachers should discourage "glorification" of death. For example, if a student is heard to say, "I wouldn't have the guts to kill myself!" the teacher can respond, "Suicide is not a brave act! It is far more courageous to go on living and face your problems each day as you and I do." Help students separate reality from fantasy and demythologize the suicide act. Inform students of the availability of crisis team and counselors at school at any time during the school day. Inform them of community resources for mental health. It is helpful to distribute a written list of names, numbers, and addresses of resources. [The Grief Recovery Institute offers a national toll-free helpline at 1-800-445-4808, Monday through Friday from 9:00 A.M. to 5:00 P.M. Pacific Standard Time.] Reassure students that any adult in the building is available to help in an emergency and is willing to listen. Members of the crisis team need to be consulted about any problems. Ask students to be supportive of one another and to escort any friend who is upset to a member of the crisis team or to the crisis center. Encourage students to discuss their feelings with their parents.

5. Announcement to be made by principal: "We regret to inform you of the news that we have received.

[Student's name], a student in [grade], has died. We will inform you about funeral arrangements when we receive them. At this time we want to extend our prayers and sympathy to the family and friends of [student's name]."

6. Short crisis team meeting after school[1]

While it's important to assure teens that grief is normal, any emotion can be taken to dangerous extremes. Intense grief that isn't resolved within one year is not "good grief." West Noble provided teachers with a list of symptoms of destructive grief with instructions to refer such students to the counseling office.

Dr. Gary Collins lists several danger signs that we need to be aware of as we work with grieving teens.[2]

Among the most prevalent indications of pathological grief are the mourner's
- increasing conviction that he or she is no longer valuable as a person;
- tendency to speak of the deceased in present tense
- subtle or open threats of self-destruction [see chapter 8 for warning signs of suicidal tendencies]
- antisocial behavior
- excessive hostility, moodiness, or guilt
- excessive drinking or drug abuse
- complete withdrawal and refusal to interact with others
- impulsivity
- persisting psychosomatic illnesses
- veneration of objects that remind one of the deceased and link the mourner with the deceased
- preoccupation with the dead person
- refusal to change the deceased's room, or to dispose of his or her clothing and other possessions
- extreme emotional expression

- a resistance to any offers of counseling or other help
- stoic refusal to show emotion or to appear affected by the loss (this usually indicates denial and avoidance of grief)
- intense busyness and unusual hyperactivity

Collins suggests that these people suffering "pathological grief" be led through "re-grief: a re-experiencing of the grief process in order to free the counselee from his or her bondage to the deceased."[3] By going back to the time of death and working through the mourning process with the teen, we can help him or her avoid some of the denial and avoidance mechanism put in place as a shield against grief.

Marge felt that the corporation's plan worked well. "The deaths really hurt all of us—staff and students alike. It was really rough, but I think we did the right thing by not cancelling school. It's always better to grieve together.

"Now, a month later, I think we're on schedule with the mourning process. The students aren't afraid to talk about the death and still mention the three missing students' names. Probably five to ten are still struggling with depression, not sleeping well, or visiting the graves frequently, but we have a regular, ongoing support group for them and any other students who need to talk about the deaths.

"One of the hardest adjustments was the empty seat. It's always a strong reminder of the death. In fact, one student wouldn't go to class because he sat next to the empty seat. I think the teacher handled it well. She moved it to the back and said, 'This was Larry's seat. We're going to move it to the back, and everyone else move up in the row.'"

Before I left Marge's office, I asked, "Would you do anything differently?"

"We held a memorial service, where a pastor spoke

about the grief process, during first period Monday after the accident on Friday night. We then gave the students the option of staying to talk with counselors and clergy spread throughout the auditorium or to go back to class. Probably fifty out of six hundred stayed to talk and hug and cry.

"I think it would have been better to have *everyone* stay for ten minutes. It didn't seem like there was time for closure.

"The tragedy brought people closer together and made them more responsive to each other. Barriers broke down between groups that didn't like each other. Now they were talking to each other and hugging one another."

Notes

Introduction

1. Jim Watkins, *Sex Is Not a Four-Letter Word* (Wheaton, Ill.: Tyndale House Publishers, Inc., 1991).

Chapter 1. How Many Teens Die Each Year?

1. J. C. Willke, *Abortion: Questions and Answers* (Cincinnati: Hayes Publishing Co., Inc., 1985), 76.

2. Is abortion really death before birth? It depends on how you define *life* and *death*. For instance, the Gulf War of 1991 was won without one bomb being dropped or one enemy soldier killed. Instead, military spokespeople informed us that "ordnance" were delivered and enemy forces "neutralized." In the same waltz of words, the pro-abortionists argue that no babies have been killed as a result of legalized abortion. Instead women have been given a "choice" in the health of "their" bodies. But is pro-choice pro-truth? Let's look at some of their arguments:

    Myth #1: "'Fetal tissue' is no more a human being than a bolt is a Buick." Those who argue that abortion does not kill human life must have skipped high-school biology and never picked up a medical book, or else they are deliberately lying. Virtually every secular medical book and even a senate hearing declare human life begins the instant of conception.

    A split second after conception, this one-celled, forty-six-chromosomed human being has everything it needs to grow into an adult human except time. It's not a blueprint of a human being. It's not a part of a human being. It *is* a human being. Never has a bolt grown into a Buick!

Because words are so important in this debate, Dr. Jack Willke, former director of the National Right to Life, warns pro-lifers to avoid emotion-laden words such as *murder* and *baby.* He urges the use of *kill* and *human life.* Pro-choicers can engage in wordplay arguing that a "baby" is not "murdered," but cannot refute—with any scientific credibility—that abortions do indeed kill human life.

A close cousin to the "it's not human life" argument is . . .

Myth #2: "A woman has a right to choose what she will do with her own body." Again, this pro-choice/pro-abortion argument reveals ignorance of human physiology or, again, the perpetuation of a deliberate lie.

The life growing within the mother is not her body. It has a very different chromosome structure with a separate circulatory system and often a different blood type. There's even a fifty-fifty chance that it's a different gender!

From a medical perspective, then, an abortion kills human life.

3. *Statistical Abstract of the United States: The National Data Book* (Washington, D.C.: U.S. Department of Commerce Economics and Statistical Administration, 1991).

Chapter 2. Is Death Like It Is on TV and in the Movies?

1. "Rust unto Rust," *People Weekly* (21 Sept. 1992): 148.

2. Quoted in the video "Rising to the Challenge" (Arlington, Va.: Parents Music Resource Center, 1988).

3. Ibid.

4. Quoted by Sally Lodge in "Read 'em and Weep," *Publishers Weekly* (6 April 1992): 23.

Chapter 3. What's the Cause of Death?

1. Two interesting studies are found in the following: Sharon Begley, "The Search for the Fountain of Youth," *Newsweek,*

5 March 1990, 44–48; and Stuart M. Berger, *Forever Young* (New York: William Morrow and Company, Inc., 1989), 31–43.

Chapter 4. Who Decides Who Dies?

1. While many Christians support capital punishment, I can find no basis for such a position in the New Testament. Under Old Testament Law, murder (Numbers 35:16) and rape (Deuteronomy 22:25) were, in fact, grounds for execution. However, to be consistent, if we use the Old Testament as "support" for capital punishment, we must support execution for *all* offenses it lists as "capital": adultery (Leviticus 20:10), homosexual behavior (Leviticus 20:13), kid-napping (Exodus 21:16), occult practices (Exodus 22:18), not observing the Sabbath (Numbers 15:32–36), striking or slandering a parent (Exodus 21:15, 17), and theft (Zechariah 5:4). Who would be left to flip the switch?

   Under New Testament grace, Christ took our "capital punishment" required under the Law:

   > When we were utterly helpless, with no way of escape, Christ came at just the right time and died for us sinners who had no use for him. . . . But God showed his great love for us by sending Christ to die for us while we were still sinners. And since by his blood he did all this for us as sinners, how much more will he do for us now that he has declared us not guilty? Now he will save us from all God's wrath to come. . . .
   >
   > Well then, are God's laws and God's promises against each other? Of course not! If we could be saved by his laws, then God would not have had to give us a different way to get out of the grip of sin—for the Scriptures insist we are all its prisoners. The only way out is through faith in Jesus Christ; the way of escape is open to all who believe him. (Romans 5:6, 8-9; Galatians 3:21-22)

   If we still lived under Old Testament Law—not grace—then the following people should have been executed:

- The woman at the well (John 4:1-42), who was guilty of adultery.
- The woman caught in the act of adultery (John 8:1-11).
- The Christians in Corinth, who were formerly "sexually immoral," "idolators," "adulterers," "male prostitutes," "homosexual offenders," and "thieves" (1 Corinthians 6:9-11, NIV)—all of whom committed capital offenses by Old Testament standards.
- Every one of us! "Yes, all have sinned; all fall short of God's glorious ideal. . . . For the wages of sin is death, but the free gift of God is eternal life through Jesus Christ our Lord" (Romans 3:23; 6:23).

   While I can't find any justification for capital punishment in the New Testament (with the exception of God's punishment of unbelievers on Judgment Day), I do find many passages that warn against judging others, not showing mercy, and mistreating prisoners (Matthew 5:7, 44; 7:2; 25:39-40, 44-45).

2. Arminians tend to emphasize free will in their theology and have many Scriptures to back up their claims. Calvinists stress God's supreme power in their doctrine, and they too have a biblical basis. That's why I label myself a "Cal-minian." I can see the arguments for both sides, even though I can't humanly harmonize the two.

Chapter 5. What Are Some Ways to Avoid Death?

1. Stuart M. Berger, *Forever Young* (New York: William Morrow and Company, Inc., 1989), 19.

2. Ibid.

3. Jeffery R. M. Kuntz, *The American Medical Association Family Medical Guide* (New York: Random House, 1982), 16-17.

4. Quoted in James N. Watkins, *Devotional Pursuits* (Kansas City, Mo.: Beacon Hill, 1986), 40.

5. Quoted by Bryce J. Christensen in "Critically Ill: The Family and Health Care in America," *Journal of the American Family Association* (June 1992): 12-13.

6. Ibid.

7. Ibid.

Chapter 6. How Can a Person Deal with Accidents and Terminal Illness?

1. Elisabeth Kubler-Ross, *On Death and Dying* (New York: Macmillan, 1969).

2. Mary Fran Hazinki, *Nursing Care for the Critically Ill Child* (Mosby Yearbooks, Inc., 1992), 42.

3. Elisabeth Kubler-Ross, *Questions and Answers on Death and Dying* (New York: Macmillan, 1974), 3.

4. J. Kerby Anderson, *Life, Death & Beyond* (Grand Rapids: Zondervan, 1980), 26.

5. James C. Dobson and Gary L. Bauer, *Children at Risk* (Dallas: Word, 1990), 147.

6. Dobson and Bauer, *Children,* 146.

7. Daniel Callahan, *Setting Limits* (New York: Simon & Schuster, 1987).

8. An excellent resource on the issues of abortion and euthanasia is Francis A. Schaeffer and C. Everett Koop's *Whatever Happened to the Human Race* (Old Tappan, N.J.: Fleming H. Revell Co., 1979).

Chapter 7. How Can a Person Deal with Murder?

1. Lee Sauer, "Former Satanist Proclaims He's a Christian," *The News-Sun* (3 March 1992): 1.

Chapter 8. How Can a Person Deal with Suicide?

1. An excellent resource book is Melody Beattie's *A Reason to Live* (Wheaton, Ill.: Tyndale House Publishers, Inc., 1991).

Chapter 11. When Does It Stop Hurting?

1. Robert B. White and Leroy T. Gatman, "The Three Stages of Grief" in *Death & Dying: Opposing Viewpoints* (St. Paul, Minn.: Greenhaven Press, 1980), 95-98.

2. C. S. Lewis, *A Grief Observed* (New York: Bantam Books, 1961), 66–67.

Chapter 12. Can You Ever Really Be Prepared for Death?

1. Harold Kushner, *When All You Ever Wanted Isn't Enough* (Tuscaloosa: G. K. Hall Publishing of Alabama, 1987), 156.

2. Joyce Landorf, *Mourning Song* (Old Tappan, N.J.: Fleming H. Revell Co., 1974), 18.

3. Concern for the Dying, 250 West 57th Street, New York, NY 10019. I would change the words *physical or mental disability* to read "an incurable terminal illness," or something similar. "Physical disability" is far too vague for me, and there are some who probably could argue that I'm "mentally disabled."

4. Scot Tuttle, Procurement Transplant Coordinator, Indiana Organ Procurement Organization, Inc., 719 Indiana Ave., Indianapolis, IN 46202, Phone 1-800-356-7757, January 28, 1992.

Chapter 14. Can Your Soul Leave Your Body before You're Dead?

1. Quoted in Anderson, *Death & Beyond,* 89.

2. Ibid., 87.

3. Ibid., 73.

4. Ibid., 100.

Chapter 15. Are There Really Such Things as Ghosts?

1. Quoted in James N. Watkins, *Devotional Pursuits* (Kansas City, Mo.: Beacon Hill Press, 1986), 29.

2. Daniel Cohen, *The Encyclopedia of Ghosts* (New York: Dorset Press, 1984), 202.

3. Danny Korem and Paul Meier, *The Fakers: Exploding the Myths of the Supernatural* (Old Tappan, N.J.: Fleming H. Revell Co., 1980), 101.

258

Chapter 16. Can You Talk to the Dead?

1. Korem and Meier, *The Fakers,* 69.

2. Ibid., 72.

Chapter 17. Do You Really Come Back as Someone Else? **259**

1. F. LaGard Smith, *Out on a Broken Limb: A Response to Shirley MacLaine* (Eugene, Oreg.: Harvest House Publishers, 1985), 33.

2. Ibid.

3. Ibid., 35.

4. Sylvia Cranston and Carey Williams, *Reincarnation: A New Horizon in Science, Religion, and Society* (New York: Harmony, 1984), 23.

5. Quoted by Jess Stearn in *Intimates through Time: The Life Story of Edgar Cayce and His Companions through the Ages* (San Francisco: Harper & Row, 1989), 13.

6. Cranston and Williams, *Reincarnation,* 7.

7. James Watkins, *Should a Christian Wear Purple Sweat Socks?* (Indianapolis: Wesley Press, 1987), 23.

8. Stearn, *Edgar Cayce,* 36.

Chapter 18. What If This Christianity Stuff Isn't Real?

1. C. S. Lewis, *Mere Christianity* (New York: Macmillan, 1964), 40-41.

2. This section adapted from a drama in James and Lois Watkins's forthcoming book, *Characters* (Kansas City, Mo.: Lillenas Publishing Company, 1993), 48–57.

3. Stoner's unbelievable odds were verified as accurate by the executive council of the American Scientific Affiliation.

4. Wilbur M. Smith, *Therefore Stand: Christian Apologetics* (Grand Rapids: Kregel Publications, 1965), 386.

5. Schaeffer and Koop, *Human Race,* 159-160.

6. Josh McDowell, *Evidence That Demands a Verdict* (San Bernadino, Calif.: Campus Crusade for Christ, Inc., 1972), 2.

7. Sir Frederick Kenyon, *The Bible and Archeology* (New York: Harper and Row, 1940), 288.

8. Robert Dick Wilson, "What Is an Expert?" *The Bible League Quarterly* (1955).

9. Josh McDowell, *More Than a Carpenter* (Wheaton, Ill.: Tyndale House Publishers, Inc., 1977), 73.

Chapter 19. Is There Really a Heaven?

1. Laurice Elehwany and Patricia Hermes, *My Girl* (New York: Pocket Books, 1991), 106–107.

2. For example, see 1 Thessalonians 5:23.

3. For example, see Job 14:10.

4. The word *sheol* is found in sixty-five different passages throughout the Old Testament in such places as Genesis 37:35, Numbers 16:30, and Psalm 16:10. The King James Version of the Bible mistakenly translates the word *sheol* as both "the grave" and "hell." *Grave* and *hell* are two different words in the original Hebrew. In the Old Testament, "the grave" is the final resting place for bodies, but not for souls.

Chapter 20. Is There Really a Hell?

1. James Watkins, *The Persuasive Person* (Indianapolis: Wesley Press, 1987), 99.

2. John P. O'Connel, ed., *The Catholic Dictionary* (Chicago: The Catholic Press, Inc., 1955), 196.

Appendix A

1. Elizabeth Richter, *Losing Someone You Love* (New York: G. P. Putnam's Sons, 1986), 10.

2. Amy Hillyard Jensen, *Healing Grief* (Medic Publishing Co., 1980), 15.

Appendix B

1. Part of the crisis plan was drawn from the writings of J. Salanto.

2. Gary Collins, *Christian Counseling: A Comprehensive Guide* (Waco, Tex.: Word Books, 1980), 418-419.

3. Ibid., 420.

Tyndale's Got Great Guidance for the Issues in Your Life!

Also by Jim Watkins:
ROMANCE   0-8423-5664-9
SEX IS NOT A FOUR-LETTER WORD   0-8423-7001-3

IF I COULD ASK GOD ONE QUESTION . . .
Greg Johnson   0-8423-1616-7

KEEPING YOUR COOL WHILE SHARING YOUR FAITH
(Coming Fall 1993!)
Greg Johnson and Susie Shellenberger   0-8423-7036-6

LETTERS TO KRISTI
Ruth Harms Calkin and Isabel Anders   0-8423-2834-3

LOOKING FOR LOVE IN ALL THE WRONG PLACES
Joe White   0-8423-3829-2

WHAT HIGH SCHOOL STUDENTS SHOULD KNOW ABOUT CREATION   0-8423-7872-3
WHAT HIGH SCHOOL STUDENTS SHOULD KNOW ABOUT EVOLUTION   0-8423-7873-1
Kenneth N. Taylor

Fantastic!
That's what teens are saying about the *Life Application Bible for Students*. Written and edited by the nation's leading youth experts, this one-of-a-kind Bible addresses the issues you face every day. Available in *The Living Bible* version, hardcover or softcover.